KT-371-361

Crisis and Change in Vocational Education and Training

192 829

Higher Education Policy Series

Changing Patterns of the Higher Education System
The Experience of Three Decades
Ulrich Teichler
ISBN 1 85302 507 0
Higher Education Policy Series 5

Evaluating Higher Education
Edited by Maurice Kogan
ISBN 1 85302 510 0
Higher Education Policy Series 6

**Governmental Strategies
and Innovation in Higher Education**
Edited by Frans van Vught
ISBN 1 85302 513 5
Higher Education Policy Series 7

Self-Regulation in Higher Education
A Multi-National Perspective
on Collaborative Systems of Quality
Assurance and Control
H.R. Kells
ISBN 1 85302 528 3
Higher Education Policy Series 15

Higher Education in Europe
Edited by Claudius Gellert
ISBN 1 85302 529 1
Higher Education Policy Series 16

Students, Courses and Jobs
The Relationship Between Higher
Education and the Labour Market
*J L Brennan, E S Lyon, P A McGeevor
and K Murray*
ISBN 1 85302 538 0
Higher Education Policy Series 21

**Innovation and Adaptation
in Higher Education**
The Changing Conditions of Advanced
Teaching and Learning in Europe
Edited by Claudius Gellert
ISBN 1 85302 535 6
Higher Education Policy Series 22

**Assessing Quality in Further
and Higher Education**
Allan Ashworth and Roger Harvey
ISBN 85302 539 9
Higher Education Policy Series 24

Are Professors Professional?
The Organisation of University
Examinations
David Warren Piper
ISBN 1 85302 540 2
Higher Education Policy Series 25

Information Technology
Issues for Higher Education Management
*Gordon M Bull, Carry Dallinga-Hunter,
Yves Epelboin, Edgar Frackmann
and Dennis Jennings*
ISBN 1 85302 542 9
Higher Education Policy Series 26

Staffing Higher Education
Meeting New Challenges
*Maurice Kogan, Elaine El-Khawas
and Ingrid Moses*
ISBN 1 85302 541 0
Higher Education Policy Series 27

**Academic Mobilty
in a Changing World**
Regional and Global Trends
*Peggy Blumenthal, Craufurd Goodwin,
Alan Smith and Ulrich Teichler*
ISBN 1 85302 545 3
Higher Education Policy Series 29

Improvement and Accountability
Navigating Between Scylla
and Charybdis
A I Vroeijenstijn
ISBN 1 85302 546 1
Higher Education Policy Series 30

**Goals and Purposes of Higher
Education in the 21st Century**
Edited by Arnold Burgen
ISBN 1 85302 547 X
Higher Education Policy Series 32

Higher Education in Ireland
North and South
Robert Osborne
ISBN 1 85302 379 5
Higher Education Policy Series 33

Study Abroad and Early Career
Experiences of Former
ERASMUS Students
Freidhelm Maiworm and Ulrich Teichler
ISBN 1 85302 378 7
Higher Education Policy Series 35

**Standards and Quality
in Higher Education**
*Edited by John Brennan, Peter de Vries
and Ruth Williams*
ISBN 1 85302 423 6
Higher Education Policy Series 37

Higher Education Policy Series 36

Crisis and Change in Vocational Education and Training

Geoffrey Elliott

Foreword by Dr Ernest Theodossin

NORWICH CITY COLLEGE LIBRARY		
Stock No.	192829	
Class	374 ELL	
Cat.	Proc.	

Jessica Kingsley Publishers
London and Bristol, Pennsylvania

All rights reserved. No paragraph of this publication may be reproduced, copied or transmitted save with written permission or in accordance with the provisions of the Copyright Act 1956 (as amended), or under the terms of any licence permitting limited copying issued by the Copyright Licensing Agency, 33–34 Alfred Place, London WC1E 7DP. Any person who does any unauthorised act in relation to this publication may be liable to criminal prosecution and civil claims for damages.

The right of Geoffrey Elliott to be identified as author of this work has been asserted by him in accordance with the Copyright, Designs and Patents Act 1988.

First published in the United Kingdom in 1996 by
Jessica Kingsley Publishers Ltd
116 Pentonville Road
London N1 9JB, England
and
1900 Frost Road, Suite 101
Bristol, PA 19007, U S A

Copyright © 1996 Dr Geoffrey Elliott

Foreword copyright © 1996 Dr Ernest Theodossin

Library of Congress Cataloging in Publication Data
A CIP catalogue record for this book is available
from the Library of Congress

British Library Cataloguing in Publication Data
Elliott, Geoffrey
Crisis and Change in Vocational Education and Training.
(Higher education policy ; 36)
1. Higher education and state 2. State aid to higher
education 3. Education, Higher
I. Title
379.1'18

ISBN 1-85302-393-0

Printed and Bound in Great Britain by
Cromwell Press, Melksham, Wiltshire

Contents

List of Figures

Foreword

Like much of the public-sector, further education (FE) has been the focus of radical transformation during the past 15 years. The resulting changes have been (and are continuing to be) driven top-down via Government policy initiatives. It is then college managers who are left to operationalise the central vision at local level, even though many of them lack the background and experience to carry out requisite hatchet work or to drive through unswerving compliance.

Despite inevitable protest, startling metamorphoses abound. FE colleges have been propelled into the market-place and encouraged to compete with one another. They have been taken away from local authorities and turned into corporations whose control over their destinies is in practice much more constrained than political rhetoric once claimed. Their funding is now administered from a central agency, with cash (and its withholding) as the means of coercing acquiescence and with a substantial number of colleges finding it difficult to balance their books. And FE establishments are subjected to rigorous external inspection: information about their successes and failures is published for the scrutiny of intending customers. The number of league tables grows. By any definition, these kinds of changes are dramatic. Only a few years ago they would have been unimaginable.

How are lecturers at the proverbial chalk face coping with such transformations? How do people to whom these changes are happening come to terms with a world in which their values and expectations are being not so much challenged as swept aside?

Geoffrey Elliott's book starts with the assertion that the English vocational education and training system is in crisis, a judgement which ministers and central agencies would certainly deny but with which few college lecturers would not feel some sympathy. The great strength of his book is that it focuses in depth and detail upon a case study involving a small group of full-time creative arts lecturers in an FE college. In one way these people are untypical of the popular view of FE lecturers: their work does not link easily with factories, offices, restaurants, hairdressing salons or nursing homes, but neither are they academics who might be considered inevitable opponents of the market-place paradigm. Rather they are professionals whose expertise forms a bridge between the worlds of art/creativity and commerce, and who are 'not resistant to business methods and practices per se'.

The book draws upon the reflective practitioner model of teaching and employs participant observation techniques for collecting data. The result is a series of illuminating insights (often rendered in their own words) into the conflict and tensions of professionals attempting to balance the demands of students and managers, while the latter seek to juggle the needs of colleagues with the pressure to do still more with even less and to measure the consequences.

In 1996 the book is very timely. Although the research underlying it precedes many current conflicts (new contracts, strikes, redundancy, mergers), the basic dilemmas persist. As the management echelon is thinned out and as colleges seek to increase productivity amidst shrinking resources, more and more is being demanded of main stream lecturers, so research which focuses on the bottom-up view is essential reading for anyone seeking to manage the new world of FE. One of Dr Elliott's main conclusions, the need to by-pass 'managerialist strategies in favour of a strategy of empowerment of their lecturing staff', is certainly prescient of recent developments such as case-loading, so all hope is not lost. In the end, when ministers have gone on to better things or the back benches, whether educational policy changes prove beneficial depends on students and teachers.

Dr Ernest Theodossin
Further Education Development Agency

Preface

This book is written at a time when vocational education and training is undergoing radical and deepseated structural change, from both within and without. It is a case study located within the FE sector, which presents the experience and perceptions of the lecturers in one department of a large urban FE College. The fieldwork on which the case study is based took place during the period immediately following the incorporation of the FE sector, when colleges were prised away from the local authorities in which they were situated and became corporate independent institutions whose control was vested in newly constituted governing bodies which strongly represented local employer interests.

The study focuses upon the impact of government policy and college procedures upon the lecturers' practice, as revealed through a variety of sources including observations, conversations, meetings and in-depth qualitative interviews. It traces the effects of the introduction of formal quality systems and quantitative performance indicators into the college, and the resulting tensions between lecturers and senior college managers over resourcing, management styles and practices.

The study has its origins in work done towards a higher degree. I am particularly grateful to Dr Valerie Hall, EdD Programme Co-ordinator, University of Bristol School of Education, and to Dr Michael Crossley, who supervised the dissertation upon which the book is based and is co-author of one of the published papers to have arisen out of the study.

Some of the material in the chapters which follow has appeared in papers published in the last two years, and I am therefore grateful to the editors and to the anonymous referees of the following specialist Education journals: *Educational Man-*

agement and Administration, Education Today, Vocational Education and Training.

My grateful thanks are also due to colleagues who have found the time within their already busy schedules to comment in detail upon drafts of chapters.

I owe a special debt to my father, Charles A Elliott FLA, for proofreading and preparing the indexes for this book.

This book is dedicated with love and gratitude to mum and dad, my wife Trudi, and my two sons Sam and Joe.

Introduction

It is my view that the English vocational education and training (VET) system is in crisis as a result of Government reforms which have been misguided in intention and contradictory in outcome. This claim is explored in this book in light of the findings of a study of a group of lecturers who work in the English Further Education (FE) sector. The book focuses upon the radical Conservative education and training policies of the present administration and examines how these are realised within one department of a college in the English FE sector. This study gives a voice to this group of practitioners, who reveal in a frank and direct way their beliefs and concerns on a range of learning, teaching and management issues. If these issues are recognised in other educational contexts, and in other countries, then the book will, I hope, be informative and relevant to a wider readership and its implications may resonate beyond the English FE sector from which its findings are drawn.

The FE sector in England is undoubtedly a significant destination for government resources. During the academic year 1993–4, £2 billion was spent on educational provision for 3 million students in 464 colleges in the sector throughout England and Wales. At the time of writing, funding has risen to over £3 billion. Given its size, its budget, and the range of provision, it is perhaps not surprising that the FE sector has consistently been characterised in the education management literature as one of high diversity and complexity (e.g. Pratley 1980; Baker 1989; Gray 1992). In the 1970s, the range of available FE provision was described as a 'maze' (Fowler 1973). In the 1980s, Twyman (1985, p.329–30) depicted the FE sector as 'in the main, one of fragmentation, confusion, complexity and competition'. In the 1990s, complexity remains a key characteristic of the sector. Responsibility for FE has until recently been shared between the government Education and Employment Departments, described by Waitt (Ed. 1980, p.207) as a 'complex and confused situation'.

The confusion may well have been fuelled in part by the political necessity to impose a succession of different employment training schemes in response to the growing youth unemployment from the 1970s. The various schemes, including Youth Opportunity Schemes and Youth Training Schemes, followed the reorganisation of vocational and industrial training within the Employment and Training Act 1973 – which also set up the Manpower Services Commission, which itself funded a considerable amount of FE provision.

A further major factor has been the plethora of awarding bodies offering separately developed, differently structured, and non-interlocking qualifications. It was in order to overcome this fragmentation, described as 'a jungle of qualifications' (Hall 1987), that government initiated the review of vocational qualifications in 1985, which led to the development of the National Vocational Qualification framework. In its wake, the National Council for Vocational Qualifications (NCVQ) commissioned the development of the General National Vocational Qualification (GNVQ), which has now taken a firm hold with 250 thousand registered students in 1994–5 in colleges and, increasingly, in schools.

Closely related to the desire to reduce diversity in VET was the desire to increase efficiency within the sector. The FE provisions contained within the 1988 Education Reform Act (1988 ERA) (DES 1988a) reflected the Government's view of the direction FE should take, and it also reflected the prevailing political climate which sought less local government control and more business involvement in education.

However, despite changes in the structure and funding of the FE sector following incorporation, diversity has remained a significant feature. Governing bodies were advised that the change in status of colleges to corporate institutions would bring about 'a new form of independence, a new maturity, which brings with it new rights, duties and responsibilities' (Cuthbert 1988, p.5). FE college principals and governors found themselves in a highly competitive market-led business. Colleges were required to bid for funding for work-related FE courses to the Training and Enterprise Councils (TECs): quangos with a majority of business representatives appointed to their boards of directors. New vocational qualifications, requiring different funding, resourcing and organisational arrangements, were introduced to accompany existing ones. Alongside the various government-sponsored training schemes, and the vast number of vocational qualifications and courses, colleges provided a significant number of non-vocational and pre-vocational full-time and part-time courses, a range of special needs programmes, and specialist provision for mature students including: Access to Higher Education, Foundation Year, Return to Learn and Learning for Work courses. In addition, an increasing amount of HE work has been located within FE colleges, with the active encouragement of the HE sector and, until recently, of the government.

The foregoing comments on the diversity of the FE sector provide the context for two complementary ideas. First, that the market orientation of the FE sector came about gradually – rather than suddenly and unexpectedly, as is often implied in the literature. The multiplicity of bodies with the potential to influence the FE curriculum – including government, local education authorities (LEAs), Further Education Funding Council, Training and Enterprise Councils (TECs), NCVQ, awarding bodies, students, parents, lecturers, college managers, governors and other educational sectors – each played a part in contributing to an enduring diversity and complexity. The influence of factors usually associated with the market in education – including performance indicators, accountability, and vocationalism – have been key features of the FE sector since the early 1980s. The 1992 Further and Higher Education Act (DES 1992) is often described by commentators as revolutionary, in that it is assumed, of itself, to have brought about a shift from a democratic to a market model of FE. For practitioners at least, the development of a market-led conception of FE is perhaps better characterised as evolutionary. Its antecedents can be found in the broad collectivity of reforms across all educational sectors brought about by preceding government legislation, associated government sponsored reports, and an increasing inclination within the sector itself to provide a responsive service to a wide range of customers and clients (Theodossin 1989). The FE curriculum, in particular the introduction of the NCVQ framework, has been a particular focus of market demands as specified by the NCVQ employer Lead Bodies (and latterly the Occupational Standards Councils), the TECs, and other employer interest groups.

The second idea follows from the first. It is commonly assumed that the incorporation of FE has brought about major changes in the working practices of lecturers. However, it appeared to the writer working with lecturers in the FE sector that they could draw upon a repertoire of strategies to thwart attempts to impose external systemic and specific changes perceived to be at variance with their core values. This is to question the assumption that lecturers respond unthinkingly or compliantly to the contradiction of externally imposed new curricula or administrative tasks. As key stakeholders (Harvey *et al.* 1992) in the educational institution and system, the lecturers in the case study around which this book is built seemed to assess and evaluate proposed changes and innovations against a benchmark described by their experience and their reflection upon past practice. At the outset of the study it was an open question how far lecturers were able to exercise this capability, within the constraints of an incorporated educational organisation within a market-led sector. One crucial aspect of the study, which links it to wider positivist/interactionist debates within social science, was the degree to which lecturers could play a decisive part in filtering and adapting externally generated reform. A key influence upon lecturers' practice appeared to be their orientation towards their students and their commitment to a student-centred style of teaching which has at its heart a belief in:

- lecturers and students working together as co-participants in the educational process
- the relevance of learning to the students' needs as well as vocational contexts
- the centrality within the curriculum of opportunities for the development of a questioning, critical and active intelligence in students.

The writer's personal experience as a lecturer in the FE sector, conversations with colleagues, discussions with other practitioners, some previous academic work in the field, and the evidence of the case study data, all support a perspective which points to the possibility of tensions between policy and practice in FE; between the reality and rhetoric of policy and its implementation. This tension is, in part, a consequence of the often contrasting and contradictory demands on, and expectations of, those who work in a complex and changing FE sector. These demands include: political pressure, through the National Targets for Education and Training (NTETS), for the 16–19 age group participation and achievement rates to match those of other European countries; calls by the FEFC for increased efficiency and inspection arrangements designed to give greater accountability; action by college managers to introduce Human Resource Management (HRM) strategies, including the imposition of the new College Employers' Forum (CEF) 'professional contract' for FE lecturers; the radical curriculum reforms necessary for the government to put in place the NCVQ framework; the everyday engagement of lecturers, support staff and students in varied and flexible teaching and learning processes.

It is the tension between these demands and the ideological orientations of FE lecturers which has provided the theme for this book. Chapter One presents a multi-level analysis of further education policy, arguing the need to take into account the historical, political and institutional context of individual action in order to access the subjective reality of educational change. Chapter Two reviews previous attempts to characterise teaching as a profession, and as occupation, work or labour. These conceptualisations are held to be limiting and to distort the complexity of teaching, and a case is presented for constructing teaching as a form of reflective practice. Chapters Three to Six present methodological issues, data and findings drawn from a case study carried out in a college of further education during its incorporation following the 1992 FHE Act. Chapter Three describes, and gives the rationale for, the qualitative methods that were chosen and employed to investigate the foreshadowed problems bearing on the tensions explored in Chapters One and Two. The next three chapters detail the results and findings of the case study, linking these to the national and institutional context of incorporation. Chapter Four presents key issues arising from the introduction into the college of BS5750 Quality Assurance procedures (BSI 1987), whilst Chapter Five explores the responses of the lecturers to the introduction of the Training and Development Lead Body (TDLB) National Vocational Qualification (NVQ) Assessor and Verifier Units (TDLB 1991), and highlights some implications of competence-based assessment of lecturers and managers in FE. Chapter Six focuses on some of the frustrations and pressures felt by the lecturer group which are held to be rooted in a tension between pedagogic and managerialist cultures which co-existed within the case study college. Chapter Seven draws together the issues raised in the study and highlights their strategic importance for college lecturers and managers. The dominance of a quantitative paradigm in educational research is noted, and it is suggested that qualitative research methodologies, such as those used in this study, have great potential to illuminate the relationship between policy and practice in further education, and to make visible the implications for the management and implementation of change. It is suggested that there is a crisis of reform in education and training, which is exemplified within the case study college.

CHAPTER ONE

The Changing Context of Further Education

The purpose of this opening chapter is to review key themes in educational policy which have a bearing upon the English FE sector. These include the debate on standards and quality, the introduction of human resource management techniques into further education and the idea of a market in education. At the level of policy making, the relationship between the 1988 Education Act and the 1992 FHE Act is shown. The chapter is also concerned to highlight the educational process itself, at the institutional and individual level. It is argued that it is equally important to take political context, institutional culture and individual subjective realities into account in understanding the changing context of FE.

The national policy context

The trend in recent years towards a radical, market orientation in education policy has been well documented (Ball 1993a; Simkins *et al.* 1992) and has been correctly identified as part of a broader movement in British government 'of which the efficiency strategy, decentralisation, performance monitoring, management information systems and devolved accountability to executive agencies are among the main pillars' (Raab 1991, p.15). This is also seen as part of 'Europe and worldwide manifestations of the market, responsiveness, entrepreneuralism and corporatism' (Parkes 1991, p.41). Such developments have been rapid but problematic, for as Hopkins (1991) has pointed out, educational institutions have encountered multiple dilemmas created by 'seemingly contradictory pressures for centralisation (i.e. increasing government control over policy and direction) on the one hand, and de-centralisation (i.e. more responsibility for implementation, resource management and evaluation at the local level) on the other' (p.1). Other writers such as Riseborough (1994, p.85) have usefully described this as a 'wholesale reconstruction' which has reshaped the structural forms, curricular, pedagogical and evaluative contents of schooling during the term of office of the present Government.

Within the FE sector less research has been carried out, but, as argued elsewhere (Elliott and Crossley 1994), there has been a marked upsurge in instrumentalist, highly specified activity, such as training for work, and the use of competence testing and quantitative performance criteria and evidence indicators. Measuring college performance had long been a hit-and-miss affair (Latcham and Birch 1985) in the hands of individual colleges and LEAs. The Department of Education and Science (DES) report *Managing Colleges Efficiently* (DES 1987) was an important milestone which shaped, in large measure, the planning framework required of FE Colleges in the 1988 ERA and introduced specific performance indicators required of all colleges as a spur to efficiency (although still 'rudimentary' [Sallis 1992]), most notably the staff/student ratio (SSR) and unit-costing. Following the 1992 FHE Act (DES 1992), which brought about FE incorporation and the setting up of the FEFC, the assessment of college performance has become a highly refined operation, upon which funding levels are dependent (FEFC 1992). Market principles are being applied to guidance services for young people through competitive tendering for careers service contracts (Watts 1993). NCVQ national standards for customer service are starting to be introduced for lecturing staff in some FE colleges (Collins 1993). The education press is replete with features with titles such as 'Academics attack market madness' (Dean 1993, p.2) and government pronouncements are unambiguous in identifying the business orientation that is required of FE colleges:

> There is nothing incompatible between education and business – each can enhance the other since both worlds have common interests. Colleges are in the market place and the successful ones can call the tune. They know they have no

captive clientele and must use the language of business for business – in order to get business. (Boswell 1994, p.4)

Standards and quality as contested values in FE

Bowe and Ball (1992), in their analysis of the relationship between education, values and the market culture, make it clear that the market 'celebrates the superiority of commercial planning and commercial purposes and forms of organisation against those of public service and social welfare' (p.53). One of the most contentious policy issues to have surfaced as a consequence of conceiving of education as a market is the concern with supposedly 'declining standards' (Pring 1992). It is argued that the preoccupation at all levels of policy formulation with 'quality assurance' is a manifestation of a market ideology, since the overwhelming concern is with quantitative performance indicators which are derived from industry (Elliott 1993), and which lead to the increasing bureaucratisation of education (McElwee 1992) and a drift towards creeping 'managerialism' (Becher and Kogan 1992).

West-Burnham (1992) is a strong advocate of the introduction of formal quality systems into educational institutions, yet he freely acknowledges the dissonance between such institutions and the industrial/commercial sector within which such quality systems were developed. He calls it 'inappropriate and foolish to propose that what worked for Japanese industry is appropriate for British industry let alone British schools' (p.14). The same point is made by the FEFC in their Quality Assessment Circular 93/28 (FEFC 1993a, p.7).

Many working in FE feel that the sector has mislaid its sense of direction, that meaning and coherence have been rooted out by a new market-orientated philosophy (Hyland 1992a). What has been lost is what Walsh (1993) calls 'the strategic relationship of education with other practices, its foundational complicity with scholarship and the arts, working life, citizenship and politics, growing up and personal relationships, the life of the spirit, etc.' (p.190). This tendency has prompted a vocal backlash in the literature, which is underpinned by an orientation towards the core values of teaching and learning. The contemporary re-emergence of the notion of a 'learning society' (Husen

1974) is consistent with the theoretical orientation underpinning the work of Stenhouse (1979a) – who consistently privileged the process of education over the extrinsic outcomes of the education process. This approach emphasises attributes such as personal development and participatory democracy, which are dependent upon 'a new moral and political order' (Ranson 1992, p.79).

Notions of education as a democratic endeavour, and the idea of ascribing a moral and ethical core values orientation to teaching, may not be thought appropriate to FE colleges, due to their association with business and training and the instrumentalist character of the employer-led qualifications which they offer. Moreover, as argued elsewhere (Elliott and Hall 1994), institutional autonomy is challenged both through the centralising tendency of central government policy towards FE and also through the increasingly widespread adoption and imposition of Human Resource Management policies and procedures for FE lecturing staff, which reinterpret their value as 'resourceful humans' (Bottery 1992, p.6).

It is important, however, not to assume that because there is a long tradition of industrial and commercial orientation within FE, there is no prospect of an alternative values orientation persisting. Many innovatory learning strategies and curriculum developments, which eschew market values, have been nurtured and developed from within the FE sector, which has been described as 'an appendage of the factory' (Brook 1970, p.183). Hyland (1994), for example, has recently highlighted the strong tradition of experiential learning methods in FE and argued that these conflict with the requirements and stipulations of the competence-based NCVQ qualifications framework.

Whilst the influence of the market upon the FE sector is no doubt strong, as shown in this study, it is not deterministic, and it is important to point out that seldom, if ever, are policies mechanistically translated into practice. The interaction between the two is complex and cannot be explained within a unidimensional model of policy and practice which assumes that policies will automatically and unproblematically become implemented. The model of policy formulation and implementation proposed by Bowe and Ball (1992) supports the adoption of a multi-level approach to policy analysis. They suggest a cycle of mutual dependence between the contexts of influence, text production and practice. One benefit of such a model is that it highlights the area of discrepancy which may exist between the ideological intentions of policy makers (shaped by interest and lobby groups), the policy text itself, and the level of implementation where adaptation of policy can take place according to the values of those who operate at the local or institutional level: 'The key point is that policy is not simply received and implemented within this arena (of practice) rather it is subject to interpretation and then "recreated"' (p.22).

This approach is further consistent with Apple's (1989) argument that to understand the roles of ideology and the state in educational policy it is necessary to 'focus on what actually happens in schools, on the agency of teachers and students, on how policies are actually made in the political area, and on what the contradicting tensions are in the reality of schools' (p.2). Apple's notion that the state consists of 'state apparatuses' (1989, p.54) is helpful in this analysis since it draws attention to the existence of the range of publicly financed institutions which together comprise the state apparatus. In particular, it is the central point that these agencies are 'neither separately nor collectively necessarily in harmony' (p.57) which draws attention to the way in which existing agencies – the local authority (LA) and Local Authorities Conciliation Settlement and Arbitration Bureau (LACSAB) – have had their control removed and new agencies are formed, such as the FEFC and the CEF, to steer the continuation and further development of FE policy.

The institutional context of policy

A significant criticism is made by Power (1992), that important aspects of the educational process may be obscured, rather than illuminated, by an over-reliance upon educational policy analysis. Her critique not only undermines policy analysis as a project in social science, but also points up that much work in the area has consistently ignored implementation at the organisational level. It is necessary for policy analysis to embrace 'what goes on inside the school gates' (p.499). To put this another way:

The implication that educational policy at the national level determines a particular pattern or mode of decision making throughout an institution should be resisted. To do so will involve managers, researchers, and others who wish to know, seeking out different understandings and differing practices within educational institutions. (Elliott 1993, p.39)

As Bines (1992) points out, experience within the schools sector 'of implementing the National Curriculum and local management of schools (LMS) suggests that our educational system may still be impervious to the more extreme aspects of government ideology; the same may yet be true of post-compulsory education' (p.116). Huberman (1973, p.42) has also emphasised the 'slow diffusion and low durability' of changes within the education system. Hall and Wallace (1993, p.112) have pointed out how other factors, such as demographics, can limit the penetration of central government policy at the local level. Riseborough (1994), in his ethnographic interview-study of two teachers in an urban working class secondary school, highlights the way in which the influence of the school context bears upon policy in practice:

> ...schooling is not epiphenomenal to the economy and polity in which policy-in-practice can be simply 'read off' from the prescriptions made by the Captains of Industry and the City, the promulgations of educational quangos or the Secretary of State for Education, etc. In-school mediations, as described, are 'value-added' social constructions of reality which are not crudely reducible to economic retrenchment and state power. The state may set the political and educational agendas but this does not mechanistically determine the lived experience of institutional life. (p.100)

All this emphasises the importance of generating theory which accommodates both the operation of the state apparatus and individuals' perceptions and experiences (Ozga 1990, p.361). Another way of putting this is that a deterministic account of the impact and penetration of education policy may well conceal the extent to which both organisational systems and human interventions may divert policies from their intended outcomes.

The historical and political context of policy

The historical context is here used to inform a perspective which links separate legislative texts by developmental or thematic threads. Little work in educational research takes adequate account of the historical context. If historical trends in policy-making are overlooked it is difficult to do other than take the motives and aims of policy-makers at face value, which would be theoretically and politically naïve. If policy analysis is in need of serious historical inputs, as Silver (1990, p.30) argues, then, as he also points out, the task is not straightforward: 'Policy-making is a process of declared intention and action, within which many processes are concealed or only dimly perceptible, and intention is one of the most impenetrable aspects of the realities which historians attempt to probe and to reconstruct' (p.140).

Where the processes of policy-making are overtly political or ideological in character, as has been widely argued (Apple 1989; Dale 1989), then the policy analyst is required to grasp the interaction between the historical and the political context.

Education policy during the 1980s and 1990s has been dominated by two pervasive ideological strands: neo-liberalism and neo-conservatism. The former draws heavily upon Hayek's notion of the superiority of the market over alternative forms of planning. The application of this strand within education by Chubb and Moe has reportedly been particularly influential amongst conservative ministers and senior civil servants (Ranson 1993, p.333). Neo-conservatism has its origin in Hobbes' notion of the dependence of society upon an externally imposed order and rule system.

These two ideological strands have been shown to be historically capable of quite broad interpretation, variously characterised as 'hard or soft', 'wet or dry', which goes some way to account for the diversity of commitment within Conservative ranks to particular Government policies, notably on Europe, introduced since 1989. It also locates the source of a central paradox of Conservative social policy reforms, which is the tension between the free market and central control. Gamble (1988) characterises the paradox at the heart of new Right philosophy as 'free economy/strong state' whilst Chitty (1989) points up the tensions between the neo-liberal doctrines of freedom of choice, individualism, the market and the neo-conservative prioritisation of social authoritarianism and strong government. And so it is, therefore, that there lies a central contradiction at the heart of the 1992 Act. Whilst setting up FE colleges as private companies, it created a structural framework which ensured their financial dependence upon a governmental quango for funding and planning purposes.

The tensions implicit in such policies are drawn out by Lawton (1992, p.17) who distinguishes four discrete ideologies which drive policy-makers: privatisation, minimalism, pluralism and comprehensive planning. Although these are located along a Right-Left continuum, all can be detected within different articulations of Conservative education policy in recent years. The issue is further complicated, in the case of educational reforms, by the tensions which are an inevitable consequence of the quasi-market. Students' and parents' choices are not free choices since places are limited, half empty schools are closed by Government decree and catchment areas are closely defined.

The policy of opting-out supposedly removed schools from what government regarded as over-prescriptive (local authority) control. Yet version one of the National Curriculum imposed a highly rigid framework, subsequently loosened somewhat following the Dearing report. It is partly such contradictions in practice – indicative of a disjuncture between rhetoric and reality – which prepares the ground for the critique of Tory education policies on the grounds that they are ideologically driven. However, policy shortcomings are commonly seen by government as failures of implementation, rather than a result of contradictions within the policies themselves.

Linkage between the 1992 FHE Act and the 1988 ERA

Against this background it is important to consider the context of government policy formulation, both historical and political. It is therefore illuminating to examine the 1992 FHE Act in the context of preceding educational reform. Dale (1989) has suggested that a broad consensus or settlement followed the 1944 Education Act, and then lasted until the period around the Great Debate in the mid-70s; this then broke down with the 1988 ERA and the introduction of explicitly consumerist policies dominated by the free market and individualistic impulses. These themes have also been explored by McNay and Ozga (1985), Chitty (1989) and Lawton (1992) amongst others. Education policies developed during the 1980s and 1990s were ideologically removed from former policies which were the outcome of a pluralistic system of policy making in which teachers, the unions and the LEAs played the major role (White and Crump 1993, p.421). However, it is beyond the scope of this chapter to demonstrate this shift in detail. The point is well made by Ball (1990): 'The education policies of Thatcherism have involved a total reworking of the ideological terrain of educational politics and the orientation of policy making is now towards the consumers of education – parents and industrialists – the producer lobbies are almost totally excluded' (p.8).

Accepting that this ideological shift has taken place, the issue here is to demonstrate the linkage, in terms of the determination of the control of educational systems, between the 1992 FHE Act and 1988 ERA, in order to reveal the system-changing agenda (McDonnell and Elmore 1991) of the former.

The 1988 ERA set the seal on the policy of encouraging schools to opt out of local education authority control. The 1988 ERA also had a major impact on the post-compulsory sector through the incorporation of higher education colleges and polytechnics as private limited companies in their own right with exempt charity status. HE institutions were now to be totally responsible for the management of their own finance, estates and personnel arrangements, and polytechnics and HE colleges were to be entitled to apply to the Privy Council to become 'new' universities. Although the 1988 ERA focused primarily upon the school and HE sectors, it significantly prepared the ground for the later incorporation of FE colleges. It not only delegated financial and other managerial powers to governing bodies of colleges, but, crucially, determined the composition of FE college governing bodies, privileging business and industry members (minimum 50% of the total) and reducing local authority members (maximum 20% of the total).

The incrementalism which had hitherto characterised government policy toward FE ended with the 1988 ERA. Once government had decided to rationalise and take direct control of FE, the extension to the sector of the principle of opting-out became a matter of timing. The policy direction was clearly established across the public sector. In the health service, the creation of health service trusts applied the principle to medical units; in local authorities, compulsory competitive tendering forced the privatisation of many council services; in the prison service, private companies bid competitively for contracts to run state prisons and secure units.

The 1992 FHE Act: system-changing legislation

It is important for an understanding of the importance of the presentation of policy by government to note that LEAs are nowhere directly criticised in the 1991 White Paper (DES 1991). Nor is there a suggestion that they have not carried out their role effectively in the past. However, where the White Paper suggests that the proposed changes will give colleges greater freedom, the only conclusion that can reasonably be drawn from the policy as text is that the intention was to give greater freedom for colleges from the LEA.

Three years after incorporation, there appear to be at least five major system-changing effects of the 1992 FHE Act upon the FE sector:

- It overturned the LEA, using the rationale that this was necessary in order to ensure that colleges had sufficient flexibility to respond effectively to market forces and satisfy the demands of their 'customers': students, their parents and their employers. However, in a very real sense, colleges were already responsive to their clients and succeeding in market terms by the government's own criteria (Audit Commission 1985; DES 1987).

- It finished the job started by the 1988 ERA: FE colleges would now be moved in the same direction as opted-out schools and the newly privatised polytechnics and colleges formerly within the PCFC sector.

- It applied an existing successful incorporation model to the FE sector, including the transfer of the funding function to a governmental quango (headed by the same individual).

- It considerably weakened a significant part of the schools sector by bringing school sixth form colleges into the new FE sector and under FEFC control. This has had the effect of substantially weakening some sixth form colleges by removing the support systems provided by their LEAs and forcing them to compete for funding in an environment in which they were seriously disadvantaged compared with more experienced FE colleges.

- The 1992 FHE Act enabled government to control growth and drive down costs by introducing the notion of 'convergence' of funding between colleges, by introducing steps to reduce the unit of resource within the sector, by adopting unit costing, and by rationalising sites through accommodation audits and the Hunter building survey – in order to limit capital expenditure on property and estates.

Despite the extensive coverage in the 1991 White Paper of curriculum matters (DES 1991: Chapters 1 – 4 *passim*), the foregoing suggests that the 1992 FHE Act has had, and is likely to continue to have, a greater impact at the organisational and administrative level than at the curriculum level. Of major relevance here is that the preferred governmental strategy for bringing about curriculum reform is to uncouple its administration from central departments to 'independent' bodies and individuals. The NCVQ, The National Commission, and the Dearing review of the National Curriculum are examples of this approach. Also, most of the so-called reforms of the vocational education system, including increasingly flexible arrangements in colleges for the management of learning and teaching (which were the subject of much of the 1991 White Paper), were already well in hand prior to the appearance of the White Paper. The Government review of vocational qualifications, which pointed the way to the NVQ and GNVQ framework, was in place six years earlier, and reported in 1987 (Deville 1987).

The process revealed above supports the notion suggested by Weiss (1982) that the development of policy is a search for 'a window for solutions' where 'the solution precedes the identification of the problem' (p.297) – in this case the solution being the introduction of the market over a range of public services.

It seems likely that reform of the FE sector was introduced in order to bring power to the centre in an attempt to secure central co-ordination and control of implementation. Hodkinson and Sparkes (1995) have signalled 'a new paradigm for vocational education and training (VET), based on individualism, choice and market forces' (p.189). Administrative devolution to a quango and the establishment of a quasi-market are evidence of the tensions which result from the ideological dualism of Thatcherism and the well-established policy of replacing local government functions by what has been variously described as the 'invisible' or 'dead' hand of government.

The perspective developed by McDonnell and Elmore (1991) is valuable in highlighting how analysis of forms of policy instrument can illuminate policy implementation research. The 1992 FHE Act introduced the curriculum reform which had been much heralded in the 1991 White Paper. However, the key feature of the Act was the putting into place of the final pieces of the jigsaw of organisational re-structuring which finished what had been started in the 1988 ERA by removing FE colleges completely from LEA control. Drawing upon this model, and also upon the cycle described by Bowe and Ball (1992) of policy formulation and implementation, the 'policy as text' within the 1991 White Paper is highly suggestive of a capacity-building policy instrument through its emphasis upon curricular reform. The reform of vocational education, however, was already well established and developed in FE colleges prior to the publication of the 1991 White Paper. The 'policy as practice', on the other hand, strongly points towards a system-changing policy instrument which removed FE colleges from local democratic control into central government control, through a quango created specifically for this purpose.

Competing visions and cultures in FE

This study, therefore, is informed by a multi-level approach which reflects, and gives due emphasis to, the complex interrelationship that exists between government intentions, managerial strategies and the impact of FE policy upon the organisation of teaching and learning in an FE college. To understand policy effects, the differing perspectives of the participants in educational institutions need to be taken fully into account in order to explore what Fullan (1991, p.32) calls 'the importance and meaning of the subjective reality of change'. Calling to mind the model elaborated by Getzels and Guba (1957), the starting point of this process is that of recognition of the ideographic dimension: the existence of the diverse understandings, beliefs and expectations held by staff in the institution.

Competing visions and conflicting cultures have been demonstrated to be important potential constraints to the successful management of change (Leithwood and Jantzi 1990, p.22). A key theme of management studies is the central place of culture in determining organisational excellence:

> Without exception, the dominance and coherence of culture proved to be an essential quality of the excellent companies... In these companies, people way down the line know what they are supposed to do in most situations because the handful of guiding values is crystal clear. (Peters and Waterman 1982, p.6)

The problem, however, for FE colleges is that the cultural *sine qua non* is unclear. A clear lesson to be learnt from work on the management of educational organisations is that cultural change cannot be imposed top down. The work of Cohen and March (1974) has been influential in suggesting that American post-compulsory educational institutions are organised anarchies, one of the main characteristics of which is problematic goals or 'a variety of inconsistent and ill-defined preferences' (p.109). They make the crucial point that educational organisations can only be managed if managers understand that 'Although a college or university operates within the metaphor of a political system or a hierarchical bureaucracy, the actual operation of either is considerably attenuated by the ambiguity of college goals, by the lack of clarity in educational technology, and by the transient character of many participants' (p.112).

Astuto and Clark (1986), in summarising the lessons of work on the management of educational institutions, draw out an important implication for the present study. They conclude that effective educational managers should concentrate on developing their ability to work with culture, rather than attempting to create it. This strategy acknowledges the existence of multiple cultures and highlights that some cultural elements may be counter-productive to management intentions. They urge the manager to focus upon the interpretations of organisational participants (1986, p.63). This viewpoint closely follows that of Weick (1982) whose loose-coupling model of educational organ-

isations warns managers against adopting hyper-rationalist solutions: '...managers need to attend particularly to the issues of
distinction (culture) and empowerment (participation) to capture the strength of their environment and avoid its weaknesses'
(p.675).

Effective management therefore requires that full account is
taken of organisational cultures as expressions of closely held
and widely shared value systems (Deal and Kennedy 1982;
Firestone and Corbett 1988), since 'the enactment and consequences of a change strategy are contingent on these contextual
characteristics' (Firestone and Corbett 1988, p.333). Neglecting
the existence of different and various cultures of teaching (Fei-
man-Nemser and Floden 1986) reduces the likelihood of progress towards the achievement of any common organisational
culture and vision. Nor can there be any reasonable expectation
of successful management of change (cp. Everard and Morris
1990, pp.231–6; Fielden 1991).

This opening chapter has emphasised the importance of
generating theory which accommodates the operation of the
state apparatus, organisational characteristics and individuals'
perceptions and experiences (Ozga 1990, p.361). Another way of
putting this is that a deterministic account of the impact and
penetration of market-led education policy may well conceal the
extent to which organisational systems, cultures and human
interventions may divert policies from their intended outcomes.
At the same time, attention must be paid to the phenomenological critique of organisation theory to ensure that the educational
organisation is not reified at the expense of the competing
priorities of individuals (Theodossin 1982, p.3). The focus in this
book upon the practice of teaching in FE recognises, and gives
due weight to, the influence of national, institutional and individual contexts and the need to point out that FE lecturers
structure teaching and learning within the external context of
policy and the internal context of implementation by college
managers. It is important to make clear that FE lecturers' actions
have a clear cultural-political dimension.

CHAPTER TWO

The Lecturer
as a Reflective Practitioner

This chapter considers the institutional context in which lecturers work, and examines the claims that have been made for teaching as a profession, as an occupation and as a form of reflective practice. There seem to be clear philosophical and political grounds for lecturers to claim their work as reflective practice.

The organisational context of teaching

The cultural ethos of universities and colleges has shifted markedly in recent years. Radical legislation affecting the post-compulsory education sector allied to major reorganisation of the vocational curriculum and new arrangements for funding and quality assurance have combined to contribute to major changes in institutional organisation. Governing bodies are now comprised of a majority of business representatives, the funding for non-vocational courses has collapsed, and decision-making takes place within a closely coupled financial framework.

The speed and scope of change is unprecedented. It can be argued that lecturers have experienced acute loss of control of their work situation through the increased pressures of external policy and curriculum initiatives. There is a developing real tension in the sector between the management-imposed imperatives of satisfying quantitative performance indicators and lecturers' conceptions and priorities based upon their value judgements. One result of squeezing resources, increased vocationalisation of the curriculum and increasing external accountability, is that lecturers are led to engage in trading off learners' needs, course needs, and their former ideas about the nature of teaching. In many cases, lecturers' personal biographies have been built around a conception of learning and teaching which would deny the very market model they are required to implement. There is a growing climate of suspicion, which fosters distrust of initiatives such as flexible learning and work-based assessment. The fear is that such developments are purportedly introduced to serve students' needs but will be used by managers to further undermine lecturers' ownership of legitimate work. It is therefore important, in order to understand the potential for change and development in the sector, that both managers and lecturers question traditionalised and, it can be argued, outmoded notions of learning and teaching.

In dealing with organisational management, structures and the phenomenon of organisational change, it is clear that there is a very large canon of literature on the field. One reason for this is that many of the dichotomies which the study of organisation theory throws up are in fact central to the conceptualisation of social science itself: order/conflict, stability/change, co-ordination/disintegration, regulation/radical change (Burrell and Morgan 1979).

The functionalist paradigm has considerable explanatory power for the study of the management of educational organisations. In particular, open systems theory, in looking at organisational structure and its relationship to the environment, draws attention to the components of the organisation itself, its internal structures and processes and the environment outside. Closed systems theory has value in identifying relationships between elements within the organisation but is unsatisfactory to deal with the environment, since the dominant metaphor, that of the machine, overplays the role of internal operations in bringing about effectiveness (Hoy and Miskel 1989).

Open systems theory, which stresses that organisations must be adaptive to their environment to be effective, potentially holds a good deal of explanatory power for the FE sector – which frequently defines itself as responsive (Theodossin 1989) and entrepreneural (Libby and Hull 1988) in relation to its outside environment. A major attraction of the open systems approach to understanding college management structures and processes lies in its focus upon the interlocking internal and external sub-systems, their relationship to each other, their different demands and the importance of boundary transactions, recognising that an event in one can affect all the others (Turner 1990).

It is the focus of attention which is critical in understanding organisational behaviour in this context. The organisation structure, its management chart, its published pronouncements relating to its objectives, its mission statement, etc., are phenomena which relate to the organisation as a structure. On the other hand, the behaviour of practitioners and their persistence in re-working known, tried and trusted strategies when faced with new external realities, relate to process and demands to be explored in terms of 'organising as against organisation' (Scott 1981, p.119).

The notion of the organisation as a loosely-coupled system has some descriptive power in helping to characterise colleges as organisations. Pfeffer and Salancik (1978) characterise an organisation as 'a coalition of groups and interests, each attempting to obtain something from the collectivity by interacting with others, and each with its own preferences and objectives' (p.36). This notion conveys a picture of competing rationalities and unintended consequences and may help to illuminate pedagogic and managerial practices in incorporated FE colleges. However, note is taken of Willower's (1982) important point that the notion of loose-coupling is somewhat amorphous, and is used varyingly in the literature to account for both high and low levels of organisational constraint.

Complexity, diversity and ambiguity need not be interpreted as dysfunctional to the needs of the FE college, however these are defined. There is evidence to suggest that there is a direct relationship between high personal tolerance of uncertainty and ambiguity of individual managers and sensitivity to signals that indicate the possible need for change in response to an unstable environment (Turner 1991). This dimension of effective management is, interestingly, notably absent from Torrington and Weightman's model, which fails to identify any positive outcomes of anarchic management styles. However, their analysis is school-based, which may account in this case for their model's exclusive association of effectiveness with more conventional management styles (Torrington and Weightman 1989).

In an important paper, Hedberg, Nystrom and Starbuck (1976) argue that hidden benefits may ensue from unstructured contexts – in particular that 'ambiguous role definitions and amorphous communication networks help an organisation adapt to marked changes in its environment' (p.45). The argument suggests that within the tightly structured organisation there develops a network of programmed behaviours, or standardised, programmed structural responses, which reduce the organisation's direct contact with the environment, supporting conventional and predictable responses. Organisational procedures have a high tolerance to changes in external stimuli, which leads to a lower response to environmental change. Such a view confirms that organisations are best viewed as a means, not an end, by the professionals who inhabit them. By so doing, they 'avoid anchoring their satisfactions in the roles and procedures that are specific to the existing organisation, and instead they draw satisfaction from the skills and relationships that contribute to processes' (p.46).

It is therefore important for a study of the process of organisational change in FE to understand the value system and culture of those with responsibility for policy forming and policy implementation. The centrality of the professional in protecting institutional integrity has been established by Selznick (1957). Given this, an understanding of the work context of lecturers and their managers is going to be central to a research agenda which seeks to gain 'a knowledge of how people in a social situation construe it, what they see as its significant features, and how they act within it' (Greenfield 1975, p.94–95).

Teaching as a profession

Little work has been done specifically on teaching in post-compulsory education as a profession; the work in this area is predominantly school-based. Educational theory has relied heavily upon the notion of teacher professionalism in order to describe and explain teachers' educational conceptions and their view of the world (e.g. Hoyle 1969, 1980; Darling-Hammond 1989; Ozga 1992). A difficulty with the notion of profession is that it invites unhelpful comparison between different professions (Lawn 1989; Pietrasik 1987). To note that lecturers do or do not have the same degree of autonomy, status or esteem as lawyers or doctors has little more than curiosity value. A second difficulty is that the notion of teacher professionalism or professionality meets with little consensus either in the literature or amongst practitioners (Hughes 1985, p.269). It is important to recognise the 'culture-boundedness' of teacher professionalism. There are important differences in the status of teachers in the US for example (a source of much literature from Lieberman (1988) onwards), and, say, Scotland. The term is differently used and understood, dependent upon the nuance of meaning attached, when used as a noun or adjective, everyday or technical term. Another difficulty lies in reconciling both the institutional context of teaching (Hoyle 1975) and the increasing prescription and demarcation of lecturers' activities through new contractual arrangements and competence-based accreditation of assessment practice with traditional models of professionalism which centre around notions of autonomy (Dennison and Shenton 1990, p.312).

Meyer and Rowan (1988), reviewing the organisation and structure of US educational organisations, reject the notion of the professionalisation of teaching, arguing that teachers themselves do not believe it. They cite the irrelevance of teacher training as judged by teachers themselves, the lack of teacher autonomy over what teachers should teach, and the generalised locus of responsibility for planning and co-ordination, as evidence that teachers are not professionals and argue that what they term 'the myth of professionalism' has arisen because teachers have much discretion within a loosely coupled system (Weick 1988) and is maintained because it serves the requirements of public confidence and good faith in the performance of teachers and pupils (Meyer and Rowan 1988, pp.96, 106). Ozga and Lawn (1981, p.11–12) have noted the difficulty of arriving at a definition of 'professional' which is not a reflection of the value position adopted by members of leading professions themselves.

A telling case is made by Grundy (1989) in her critique of the relevance of professionalism to teaching. She argues that the self-critical, reflective practitioner must inevitably be in a different power relationship to the client than would a professional, that is a relationship which minimises control and coercion and maximises mutual respect and co-operation. Behind this view is the assumption that a professional's primary duty lies towards colleagues. This view is consistent with Illich's (1973) position that a key agenda for professionals is the defence of their profession, which can limit their commitment to those who are in receipt of their services.

Carr and Kemmis (1986) take a different view of the primary focus of professionals, which underlines the elusiveness of the term. For them, a 'distinguishing feature of professions is that the overriding commitment of their members is to the well-being of their clients' (p.8). Despite this differing emphasis on where the responsibilities of professionals lie, they also spell out 'the limited extent to which teaching, as we know it today, can legitimately be regarded as a professional activity' (p.8).

Avis (1994) criticises the notion of professionalism as applied to teachers on the grounds that 'ahistorical and essentialist notions of professionalism, as expressed in trait approaches and those which fall back upon definitions of knowledge and skill that constitute expertise', cannot address issues of social antagonism and social difference (p.65).

A looser use of the term 'professional', indicating 'commitment, self-organisation, and a certain status' (Pietrasik 1987), underlies contemporary debate on FE lecturer's terms and conditions of service (e.g. McBean 1994, p.6; NATFHE 1994a) and is implicit in the CEF so-called 'professional contract' (CEF 1993).

Hoyle (1992) has noted that 'there appears to have been a semantic shift in the connotation of *professional* as adjective and noun which has somewhat uncoupled the term from its original reference to profession' (p.5) [original emphasis]. It is the very attractiveness of some of the attributes traditionally associated with professionalism and professionality which has led many to wish to retain the link between teaching and professionalism. Some of these attributes are:

- the idea of expertise, or a job well done, as in 'a professional job'
- the idea of autonomy, which is a very powerful concept for lecturers in the context of increased centralisation of educational policy

- the idea of specialist knowledge, another powerful concept when appraisal mechanisms and accreditation procedures are held to be de-skilling lecturers
- the altruistic ideal of education for its own sake
- the idea of the exercise of critical judgement and creativity in deciding the best approach to meeting learners' needs.

Salaman (1979, p.137) presents a profile of organisation-based professionals which incorporates a number of these attributes. The value of professionality as a notion for teachers and lecturers themselves may be found in its potential to legitimate autonomy.

The slippage in the use and application of 'professional' represents a significant danger of teaching becoming marginalised as a profession in post-compulsory educational institutions where other professions and different professional values are given more status and esteem. University and college managers might legitimately reduce staffing levels and contact hours and replace lecturers with technicians, demonstrators and postgraduate students whilst at the same time claiming to serve the students' best interest in terms of 'service to the customer', 'value for money' and increased throughput – notions which can be, and frequently are, sustained by a use of the term 'professional' which is founded upon the ideology of a business efficiency ethic.

Teaching as occupation, work or labour

Occupational and work characteristics of teachers are referred to by Hodkinson (1992) and Ball (1993a). Other accounts highlight the extent to which teaching is open to influences which are held to be bureaucratising (Darling-Hammond 1989), deskilling (Ayres 1990; Hyland 1992b), de-professionalising (Trow 1993, p.21) and proletarianising (Apple 1986; Ozga and Lawn 1988). All of these factors gain a particular force when applied to lecturers in post-compulsory education. The use of competence-based education (CBE) approaches to the accreditation of lecturers, through the use of occupational standards, are argued to be evidence of this kind of trend.

Pietrasik (1987, pp.169–70) argued that teachers were turning to trade unionism to secure better pay and conditions, rather than appealing to professional status. In a school context, Lawn (1989), has argued that 'teachers' work is going to be (or already is) more clearly defined, more fragmented, more supervised and more assessed, and that teachers are losing control over it' (1989, p.154). As noted elsewhere (Elliott and Hall 1994), Human Resource Management strategies underpin a view of the labour force as an allocatable resource. Teaching qualifications of any kind have never been a pre-requisiste for lecturers in post-compulsory education, but there is a growing concern at the mandatory imposition of low-level competence-based testing procedures upon experienced lecturers (Ashworth 1992; Chown 1992; Chown and Last 1993).

Hyland (1992b) has been influential in arguing that the development and implementation of Training and Development Lead Body occupational standards for lecturers undermines the teaching role. This issue is fully explored in Chapter Five but it is important to note here that Hyland's critique of the introduction of a competence-based approach to lecturer training is largely based upon the limitation of the lecturers' role, which is implicit in the performance specifications of the TDLB Assessor and Verifier Units. He also signals the inherent danger, consequent upon functionalist occupational mapping, of producing compliant staff 'who are uncritical of change but well able to perform the tasks and duties required of them by college management' (Hyland 1992c, p.11).

Hyland then proceeds by implication to flesh out a view of what the teaching role might entail and, at the same time, what it is about the role that cannot be described by the occupational work role criteria which underlie the TDLB framework: 'The pace of change in the post-school sector in recent years has resulted in a fluid and uncertain state of affairs in which lecturers are required to be flexible, critical, reflective and knowledgeable about a vast range of curricular and organisational matters' (p.11).

In a later paper, Hyland (1993) argues for a model of lecturer professionalism based upon the notion of 'professional expertise'. The circularity of this position considerably undermines his application of the term professional in this context. In fact, the literature he cites to support his notion of 'professional expertise' in almost all cases focuses upon 'expertise' rather than '*professional* expertise'. Hyland himself acknowledges that the literature on experts points to certain common traits which 'seem particularly appropriate in relation to the "reflective practitioner" model' (p.129). Carr (1993), in his discussion of the knowledge and professionalism of teachers, similarly has recourse to the idea of the reflective practitioner to summarise what he means by professional when applied to teaching (p.253).

Rationale for a reflective practitioner model of teaching

The growth of managerialism and the demands made by policy shifts towards a mass participation system of post-compulsory education suggests that this might be an opportune moment to re-visit the nature of teaching practice. As lecturers find themselves working for managers with employment experience outside education, and who allocate resources according to business priorities, it may become more necessary for lecturers to affirm the territory of *their* expertise. Occupational standards which emphasise competences demonstrated in a designated workplace may be found to be too limiting in the way in which they circumscribe lecturers' practice, whilst viewing teaching as a profession, on the other hand, carries with it the danger of legitimising a wide range of assumptions and activities which focus attention and resources away from the teaching and learning process. Drawing upon literature from educational management, and the sociology, psychology and philosophy of education, some ground rules can be proposed for a new conceptualisation of teaching.

In order to be meaningful and valid for the practitioner, a new conceptualisation should be grounded in lecturers' own understanding and experience of their working practices – and it should adequately reflect the range of these practices – as well as their epistemological and ethical basis (Day and Pennington 1993, p.251). It should reflect a phenomenological perspective towards organisations, which recognises the centrality of understanding individual's orientations (cp. Maslow 1954), and that 'organisations are to be understood in terms of people's beliefs about their behaviour within them' (Greenfield 1975, p.83). It should also be capable of supporting theoretical and political opposition to attempts to re-define practitioners' shared educational values (Avis 1994). This last point is increasingly important in light of attempts by the CEF to apply the term 'professional' to their new restrictive and widely opposed (Uttley 1994) college lecturers' contract of employment.

A key limitation of the model of teaching as a profession is that it implies a consensus and common orientation among lecturers which the literature does not support (Little 1984; Fullan 1990; Huberman 1990). An important advantage of the concept of reflective practice over the concept of professionalism is that the former is more consistent with a micropolitical perspective, recognising the different interests, biographies, careers, priorities, subjects, status and pedagogical orientation of lecturers.

Hargreaves, in his work on contrived collegiality (1991), teacher individuality (1993a; 1993b) and balkanisation (1994), highlights the importance of taking teachers' individual differences into account in understanding the working practices and assumptions of teachers. He warns against assuming the existence of a shared culture amongst members of an organisation, arguing the possibility that 'some highly complex organisations may have no shared culture of any substance' (1991, p.50). This view is supported by Astuto and Clark (1986), who argue that some educational institutions may be 'culture light' (p.62).

A second important characteristic of the notion of reflective practice is that it is capable of encompassing moral and educational values as well as specific 'professional' practices (cp. Elliott 1989; Grace 1993). This is not insignificant at a time when educational managers are under pressure to re-define their own roles and those of their staffs, away from pedagogical orientations towards a model of professionality which has more to do with a business and market orientation which 'bespeaks a philistine simplism' (Stones 1989, p.8), or towards what Carr (1994) has called 'a technicist conception of educational professionalism focused largely on the development of superficial tricks of the trade' (1994, p.50). In circumstances where the role of the education professional may come to be re-defined by other stakeholders, then a conceptual re-orientation may be timely, since it is only through the 'grounding of our actions in our values that we can recognise the nature of the competing rationalities we face and find means of coping with them, whether as managers or as those being managed' (Bennett, Crawford and Riches 1992, p.15).

A third feature of the proposed model of reflective practice specifically addresses the criticism raised by Avis (1994) of the reflective practitioner notion presented by Schon (1983; 1987) and Elliott (1991). Avis characterises the idea of the reflective practitioner as solely concerned with '(meeting) clients, collaboration, holistic understanding and self reflection…absent however is an engagement with power, politics and difference' (p.67). He presents reflective practice as a facilitator model of teaching, similar to the role of counselling, which he claims ignores the social struggles surrounding education, and rests on the premise that professional educators really do know best, and which understands 'teaching as a neutral enterprise, only compromised by values orientated towards the educational development of all – a quasi-neutrality – that fails to address the politics involved and the very real conflicts and social antagonisms surrounding education' (1994, p.68). However, his position is quite ambiguous, since he acknowledges that whilst 'the technological rationality of traditional professionalism is deemed dysfunctional and thereby fails in its own terms,…a dynamic model of professionalism embodied in the reflective practitioner is valuable, in that it does encourage us to examine the taken for grantedness of our practice, to indulge in autocritique' (1994, p.68). In suggesting that the limitation of the reflective practitioner model is that 'it is compromised by its lack of a politics' (1994, p.68), Avis fails to recognise that reflection, critique and examining taken-for-grantedness – reflective practice in *his* terms – are essential pre-requisites for political action, either at a micro or macro level (Blase 1991, p.11; Griffiths 1993, p.158; McCulloch 1993, p.300). Indeed, it is only through reflective practice that the 'preoccupation with the personal, and the relative neglect of the social and political (which) is a chronic condition of post-modernity' (Hargreaves 1993b) can be avoided. At bottom, Avis' position is rooted in a single, rather than a multi-level, analysis of political action. He fails to acknowledge that it is necessary for individuals to adopt a reflective practice in order to draw coherent linkages between institutional and national contexts.

The model of reflective practice which underpins Freire's (1972, p.15–16) notion of 'conscientisation' fully meets Avis' objections. For Freire, conscientisation refers to the development of a critical consciousness (rather than consciousness-raising, in a patronising sense) to a level where individuals can achieve a sufficient degree of social and political awareness to understand contradictions within society and, crucially, to work to transform it. As Hargreaves (1993b) concludes: 'In what we do with teachers and in how we study teachers and their development, it is time to "get real"; to reconnect the system with the self, as part of a critical, collaborative and deeply contextual agenda for change' (p.110).

Teaching as reflective practice

It is an unfortunate and limiting characteristic of a good deal of educational research that it fails to recognise the antecedents of some of the central issues and concepts with which it deals. Thus, the idea of the reflective practitioner is often attributed to Schon (1983; 1987). Whilst there are good reasons to account for Schon's popularisation of the notion (Eraut 1995, pp.9–10), the origins of the idea go somewhat further back.

The idea of reflective practice can be demonstrated to be at the centre of British philosophical discourse, from the seventeenth-century philosopher Locke's (1690) concern with appropriate knowledge and judgement as vital to well-informed rather than ill-informed understanding, through Mill's (1843) concern with the centrality of inferential thinking to the exercise of good judgement. John Dewey (1933, pp.287–8) was the first formally to apply the idea to the educational situation. His definition of reflective thought is predicated upon its status as a conscious, voluntary and purposeful activity. Dewey believed that reflective thinking was an artistic rather than scientific endeavour and that it represented the ideal human mental state (pp.287–8), and an antidote to a restrictive preoccupation with 'those things that are immediately connected with what we want to do and get at the moment' (Dewey 1970 [1929], p.159).

Stenhouse (1979b) recognised the key role of reflective thinking for educational practitioners in arguing that what is learnt from comparative studies can 'tutor our judgement' (1979b, p.6). Schon (1983, p.62–3) develops Dewey's notion of the essential artistry involved in the intellectual process of reflecting on action. It is the *creative* dimension of reflective practice which enables practitioners to deal effectively with inconsistent or incompatible demands and which thus makes it such a powerful framework for understanding action in non-rational, unpredictable organisations.

The unpredictability of much classroom knowledge is also acknowledged by Eisner (1967, p.89), who distinguished between learning characterised by behavioural, instructional objectives and that characterised by novel or creative responses, and argues that pre-specified behaviourist approaches to learning and educational evaluation are inappropriate for the latter, since the student's behaviour cannot be specified in advance (1969, p.93).

Eisner's model of classroom knowledge as created, shared and unpredictable is evocative of the work of those, such as Freire (1972, p.44), who reject bureaucratic teaching and learning procedures in favour of a critical student-centred pedagogy. Central to this model is the notion of teacher and student as of equal status as subjects: 'the students – no longer docile listeners – are now critical co-investigators in dialogue with the teacher' (p.54). Freire contrasts this 'co-intentional' model with the prevalent 'banking' model of education where 'knowledge is a gift bestowed by those who consider themselves knowledgeable upon those whom they consider to know nothing' (p.46).

As Gore (1993, p.42) has pointed out, it is the attention which Freire pays to the elaboration of an alternative critical pedagogy, rather than the generation of abstract educational theory, which makes his contribution so valuable and potent. By re-conceptualising the task of the lecturer it is possible for the lecturer to make a significant impact upon the quality of students' educational experiences. Freire's pedagogy requires teacher and student, jointly, to engage in the educational process as partners, each having an active and valuable contribution to make within a negotiated curriculum. This approach can also be conceptualised as a 'dialectical learning relationship' (Fryer 1994, p.19). As Trow (1993) notes:

> Teaching is not an action, but a transaction; not an outcome, but a process; not a performance, but an emotional and intellectual connection between teacher and learner. Therefore it cannot be assessed as an attribute or skill of a teacher or a department, independent of the learners who have their own characteristics which affect whether and how much they learn (about what) from a particular teacher, and, indeed, how much they learn from them. (p.20)

The conception of teaching as an activity underpinned by 'core values' is a persistent one in the literature which attempts to characterise teaching and explore its key attributes. Carr (1987), for example, claims that 'a definitive feature of an *educational* practice is that it is an ethical activity undertaken in pursuit of educationally worthwhile ends' (pp.165–6). He cites Peters' argument that these ends 'are not some independently determined "good" to which educational practice is the instrumental means. Rather they define...the "principles of procedure" which constitute a practice as an educational practice and justify its description in those terms' (p.166). For Altrichter and Posch (1989) education is essentially a moral practice aimed at the realisation of values, and for Sockett (1989), more specifically, teaching is concerned with moral values such as care, courage and truth. This emphasis upon core values would, as Elliott (1989) points out, refute an 'objectives' model of curriculum development and lend weight to Stenhouse's (1980) 'process' model. In Whitehead's (1989) terms, and as action research has clearly demonstrated, the values of education are realised through educational practice, not through a prescribed and predetermined set of objectives or outcomes. Reflective practice, then, can be construed as epistemologically and ethically linked to philosophical and pedagogical traditions which assert 'that the educational character of any practice can only be made intelligible by reference to an ethical disposition to proceed according to some more or less tacit understanding of what it is to act educationally' (Carr 1987, p.166).

The focus upon core values locates the reflective practitioner model within a cultural, epistemological and essentially ethical tradition which transcends economic, political and administrative expedience (cp. Gadamer 1980, pp.249–262). Viewed through this lens, it is not difficult to see why competence-based approaches which focus upon the activity, rather than the context and worth of the action, have fuelled a powerful critique which focuses upon the extent to which CBE impoverishes the educational experience. It is the extent of the radical centralist CBE-based curriculum reforms introduced by NCVQ (Hyland 1994), and the degree to which they have undermined the core values associated with teaching and learning (Smithers 1993, pp.9–10), which has led to the most vocal critical comment. Hyland (1994, p.235) has illustrated the pervasive power and influence of the NCVQ framework and has pointed out that the CBE strategies which underpin the NCVQ framework are diametrically opposed to the conception of learning and development held within the reflective practitioner model. He argues that the development of what he calls a 'learning culture' (1994, p.242) in post-school learning requires a closer look at strategies concerned with learning *per se*, rather than performance or outcomes. In Eisner's (1967, p.89) terms, a weakness of CBE would be that it fails to distinguish between the application of a standard and the making of a judgement.

Conclusion

This chapter has surveyed notions of teaching as a profession, work, labour and occupation. These were found to be inappropriate, confusing or limiting for FE, and a rationale for the development of a reflective practitioner model of further education teaching was given. A framework for the model, which highlighted core values and was grounded in a critical pedagogy, was proposed. It is this alternative, practitioner-based model which was explored in the case study which is described in the ensuing chapters. One of the aims of the study was to extend the literature by generating FE-located theory which draws upon the areas of reflective practice and critical pedagogy, in order to offer a re-conceptualisation of lecturers' orientations to their work. A key question arising from the literature, which is central to the aims of the case study, and which was pursued within it, is: how do FE lecturers themselves define their task and what has been, or will be, the likely impact of market-led policies for FE?

CHAPTER THREE

Researching a College
Methods and Problems

This chapter describes, and gives the rationale for, the qualitative methods that were chosen and employed to investigate the foreshadowed problems identified hitherto. The limitations of the study are identified and some important arguments relating to the generalisability of the study are weighed.

Epistemology

The research methodology employed in this study was not predetermined from the outset, but was open, shaped and developed gradually, as a consequence of the writer's understanding of, and engagement with, the research problem. The focus of the study was upon lecturers' reflections upon their own practice (Schon 1983; 1987). These were viewed within the lecturers' work context. In order to access a broad range of data bearing upon the implications of policy and the interaction between lecturers and managers, a participant observation model was employed. It was, then, the nature of the research problem which determined the precise form and range of data collection and analysis.

The methods employed reflect an epistemology which privileges grounded data (Glaser and Strauss 1967). At the same time there is a strong sense in which the researcher, as a participant, brings preconceived notions, perspectives and frameworks to the research situation (Rowan and Reason 1981, pp.134–5; Hammersley 1993, p.57ff.). It would be disingenuous to attempt to deny that this is so. The high level of involvement of practitioners in their work, and the large extent to which lecturers' practice is influenced by a theoretical orientation, are both high-lighted in this study. So it is for the researcher. This chapter acknowledges the problematic tension between, on the one hand an 'open' methodological stance, which is sensitive to emerging issues and problems, and on the other, the prior assumptions and expectations which the participant brings to a study of colleagues, which can be derived from a wide range of experiences and characteristics including age, ethnicity, gender and social class.

'Foreshadowed problems' and 'progressive focusing'

A way forward, which proved productive in developing a theo-retical orientation for this study, is given by Malinowski (1922) who, in his anthropological studies of societies in the Western Pacific, developed the notion of 'foreshadowed problems': 'Pre-conceived ideas are pernicious in any scientific work, but fore-shadowed problems are the main endowment of a scientific thinker, and these problems are first revealed to the observer by his theoretical studies' (p.9).

Foreshadowed problems are issues which are identified from any source as likely to be significant. Research in the field is informed by, but crucially not determined or limited by, the foreshadowed problems. They are used to guide initial analysis. An example in this particular research is the contradictory ex-perience of those lecturers who hold what can be broadly de-scribed as a democratic, student-centred ideology; who are faced with increasingly narrow, externally imposed, technisistic, means-end curriculum models. Such problems were identified from the writer's awareness and experience of relevant and significant issues as a reflective practitioner within the FE sector, from his theoretical orientation, from the literature, and from issues encountered whilst carrying out research in post-compul-sory education. Foreshadowed problems point both to the topic of this study and suggest its potential significance in under-standing the tensions between policy and practice in FE.

Once in the field, progressive focusing gives a cumulative impetus to the research by building upon prior insights drawn from earlier data gathering to sharpen the researcher's sensitiv-ity to the social situation and the data and to refine the research instruments. Thus, in this study, questions explored with participants became more focused upon the issues which lecturers, interviewed early in the study, defined as problematic. The researcher's developing awareness, arising from an increasingly personal and committed engagement with a particular research problem, was also a crucial resource in progressive focusing.

However, the emergence of unanticipated problems, and the need to do what Johnson (1975) describes as 'defocusing field research' (p.65), required that the research design remained open during the process of the study itself. In this respect, Malinowski's (1922) distinction between preconceived ideas and foreshadowed problems was important to the study for similar reasons as he himself suggests. Foreshadowed problems allow theory and data to interact; at the same time new information and understandings may require the research to move away from the preconceived design: 'If a man sets out on an expedition, determined to prove certain hypotheses, if he is incapable of changing his views constantly and casting them off ungrudgingly under the pressure of evidence, needless to say his work will be worthless' (p.8).

Preconceived notions are powerful in that they form agendas, define frames of reference and close down alternative possibilities. In this study, all the research topics and issues were discussed freely with respondents and other participants in the college in an attempt to remain as open as possible to other arguments and ideas. Thus the foreshadowed problems were foregrounded in this study through the sharing of topic areas for discussion and exploration with the participants. Not all these foreshadowed problems proved to be significant to respondents. Others took on a greater significance than anticipated. This process of variable development of conceptual frameworks and notions offered a rich source of ideas to the researcher and, it is argued, underwrote the value of an open-ended research design for accessing participants' reflective perspectives upon their practice.

There was some progressive focusing of pertinent issues through the linear timetabling of interview sessions at monthly intervals between May 1993 and January 1994. In this way, issues highlighted as significant during the review of the literature and early data-gathering were specifically explored in detail during subsequent sessions, whilst maintaining alertness to the possibility of new pertinent issues being raised through interviews, discussions, conversations and meetings during the later stages.

Participant observation

Participant observation strategies require some explanation, since they can be variously interpreted. For example, there is more than one possible significance that can be attached to the term 'participant'. Wagner (1993) distinguishes between 'participant research' and the 'participant observation' methodology given prominence by sociologists following Pearsall (1956), Becker (1958) and Whyte (1964). The distinction is that the sociological tradition of participant observation 'refers usually to the research method of direct observation, not the prospect of occupying an official position within the organisation or group being observed' (Wagner 1993, p.4). The term 'participant' refers to the active and passive presence of the researcher among the group, in whatever capacity or role.

This consideration is important since it has a key bearing on the nature of the relationship between researcher and researched. The reader is entitled to question the exact relationship between the researcher and the group being studied, in order that s/he may assess the influences being brought to bear upon the design and methodology of the study. However, there is a primary obligation on the researcher who is carrying out a case study to honour the confidentiality of both the case study institution and those who participate in the research. Balancing the requirements of this obligation with the obligation to inform the readership of the context in which the research is carried out is not easy. What is clear, however, is that the former obligation is and must remain paramount. It is therefore necessary to require the reader to take a certain degree of information on trust. This is a problem that besets qualitative research rather more than quantitative, since the depth and detail of data provided by qualitative methods are typically very closely linked to the personal identity and biography of the respondents. It was for these reasons, therefore, that each lecturer interviewed was given the opportunity to verify, comment upon and amend where appropriate their own transcript, and to agree to its publication. Interviewees were also invited to add further comments in the light of their subsequent experiences since the study as practitioners in the case study college.

Since this research probed sensitive policy issues which had a direct bearing upon the everyday practice of the lecturers, it was crucial from the point of view of the validity of the study to establish to what extent the respondents felt able to express their feelings openly. It was argued that many factors have a bearing upon the objective to ameliorate any effect due to differences in orientation between researcher and researched. Assurances were given to all respondents regarding the confidentiality with which the data and findings would be handled and a basis of trust was established. The respondents appreciated the significance of the research for them, as its focus became clear to them during the period of the study. They were, therefore, predisposed to be willing, supportive and constructive participants. They were interested in discussing the implications of educational policy for FE and their own practice, and many have sought further opportunities to make their views known.

In addition, there was the evidence contained in the interview transcripts. The data revealed strong feelings, a willingness to discuss the roles and style of senior management, a frankness about personal success and failure, and a preponderance of critical and perceptive responses. All of this lent support to the view that the respondents were not intimidated or stifled by the interaction with the researcher.

What is not known is to what extent the respondents were led by the developing focus of the research to overplay their critical responses to the new characteristics of the FE sector and the strategies employed by senior managers. It is, however, important to bear in mind two points. First, disconfirming cases, where they occurred, were always included in the data – that is, where a lecturer expressed a view which disagreed with colleagues, or which would question the researcher's assumptions, that view was always reported in the study. Second, it is argued that it is to a degree patronising to assume that respondents were open to auto-suggestion or halo effects, rather than expressing the realities of their world as they see and experience it.

During the period of the research study, it was possible to gain access to a range of internal documents, which chiefly emanated from management, and included memoranda, letters, circulars, bulletins, file notes, policy statements, guidelines and handbooks. Observation of meetings attended by department heads and senior management also provided useful background information on the stated priorities of both groups within the college, whilst free access to the site which housed a particular staff group – those involved in creative arts – enabled observation of their meetings, as well as participation in informal conversations, lunchtime gatherings and social occasions.

Sources of data

The primary technique for the study was the qualitative, semi-structured or open-ended interview. In its questioning of the assumptions of the positivist tradition in Social Science, the open-ended interview draws upon a broad range of methodological principles (Bogdan and Biklen 1992, p.3) which focus to a greater or lesser extent upon the recording of participants' perceptions and accounts of their practice, and the work context.

Sociological research has made extensive use of the qualitative interview, or what some call the ethnographic interview (Whyte 1943; Becker *et al.* 1961; Glaser and Strauss 1967). Within this tradition, conceiving of and conducting interviews as conversations (Burgess 1984) are predicated upon the assumption that the researcher can establish a relationship of trust with respondents. Such a relationship is essential when inquiring into working practices which may be at variance with government policy and institutional guidelines.

It is acknowledged that data is available to the ethnographer through both formal and informal contact with subjects and is refined through subsequent thinking and reflection. It is, therefore, important to select data gathering methods which allow the recording of conversations and discussions, observations of dialogue, and whatever else seems to be relevant at whatever stage of the research process (Johnson 1975, pp.187, 198). At the same time, there are a number of key issues, drawn from relevant literature, personal reflection, and foreshadowed problems, about which all respondents are questioned. Hence the triangulation approach to data gathering employed in this qualitative study.

The literature on reflective practice surveyed in the previous chapter contextualises the study; it points up key issues, provides touchstones for the theoretical framework, and provides a basis for comparison between the study and other research in similar and related areas. An important consideration in the selection of theoretical constructs is their direct relevance to the research problem and their judged potential for informing a critique of current policy trends within the FE sector. As a counterbalance to the deterministic tradition within FE-located theory, the study focused instead upon a tradition which asserts the potential of the practitioner, whilst at the same time recognising and taking into account social, cultural and political influences. The limitations imposed by the relative paucity of research done on the FE sector were balanced by the freedom to apply and test theory developed within other contexts.

The focus of the study was on policy and practice within an FE college as identified and articulated by a group of full-time lecturing staff. Detailed responses were required to a range of policy and pedagogic issues. It was therefore, necessary to spend time with respondents in a variety of settings in their workplace, in order to sensitise the researcher to their concerns and to aid understanding and analysis of their responses. Additionally, access to appropriate documentation was required. The twin demands of maximising contact with subjects and access to important documentary information, can only be achieved successfully through a case study approach.

Use was made of a range of printed material – including official college documents, some of which were crucial in mapping participants' perspectives and the institutional and national contexts. Through these sources, it was possible to gain access to the public statements of managers and to establish which issues were given prominence. Other relevant documents, such as official memos, circulars, letters and ephemera, were collected. National policy documents were also used as sources of data. At the time of the study, the college was pursuing accreditation by the British Standards Institute (BSI) for its quality kitemark BS5750 (or ISO 9000), and therefore its quality manuals were a further source of data for the study.

Field notes were made of observations, interaction, meetings, ethical issues, methodological problems, schedules and unanticipated data. These notes were coded, indexed and filed, and thus became a valuable source of reference for contextualising the fieldwork data. The notes helped in the process of progressively focusing upon key issues within the college as the impact of incorporation became clear. They also served the purpose of helping to ensure that the limitations of the study (fully acknowledged and explored later in this chapter) were noted and taken into account.

The qualitative interview

This section describes how the interviews were carried out and how data was produced from them. The methodology of data analysis is discussed later.

An open-ended interview schedule was prepared with two objectives in mind. First, to focus the interviews upon the key substantive issues which had emerged from the literature review, participants' own concerns as expressed in conversations and meetings, and the writer's own reflective practice, without imposing an over-prescriptive framework. Second, to allow for the progressive focusing of questions and discussion. The schedule developed and changed during the time-scale of the interview phase to take into account ideas and points which emerged during data collection. This tiered approach, which staggers data collection and analysis, allows the researcher to engage in 'constant comparison' (Glaser and Strauss 1966, p.277) and to formulate ideas and concepts which can be applied to later data collection.

The topics covered in the interviews included: the lecturers' own career and biography, trade unions and professional associations involvement, the idea of the lecturer as a professional, and response to policy issues such as: schools opting out of local authority control; incorporation of FE; the market in education; performance indicators and quality assurance systems and procedures; human resource management; appraisal; the lecturers' philosophy of education, its development and its relationship to their practice; the TDLB awards and the role of the lecturer; the place of subject knowledge, educational values and lecturer expertise; competency and outcome-based learning; the development of their subject; modularisation; approaches to organising learning and teaching; college management practices and styles; college culture.

The interviews took place in a quiet area away from classrooms and workshops with relatively few interruptions. A relaxed atmosphere was created by the use of easy chairs, the careful timing of interviews (usually late afternoon or evening), clear explanation about the purpose of the interview and assurances about confidentiality.

Each interview lasted between one and one and a half hours. A small, unobtrusive cassette tape recorder with built-in microphone recorded the data and verbatim transcripts were made. Each interview was replayed and compared with its transcript several times to ensure accuracy. Each transcript was then printed to paper within a left hand column, leaving a right hand column for notes and observations.

The case record

A major source of evidence for this study was the transcripts of interviews with lecturers in the case study college. This evidence or 'case record' (Stenhouse 1978, p.32) is directly drawn upon in the next three chapters and has also substantially informed subsequent re-working and re-analysis of the project as a whole.

There are compelling reasons for the researcher making the case record available, 'both as grounding for his own reportage, and as a resource for communal use by the community of educational researchers' (Stenhouse 1978, p.33). The guidelines suggested by Stenhouse for presentation and availability of the case record have been followed in this instance: '...the preferred case record is an edited version of the full transcript which attempts to present the school as it is perceived by those who are participant in it' (p.34). The aim of the researcher in editing the transcript 'is not "telling it like it is"...but it is an attempt at "telling it as it feels to be in it", that is to say, telling it as it phenomenologically is' (p.34). This case study, therefore, reflects the archetype proposed by Stenhouse and can be characterised as: 'an interpretive presentation and discussion of the case, resting upon, quoting and citing the case record for its justification' (p.37).

The interview group

All the staff who participated were on full-time contracts within a single department of the college, creative arts, when the interviews were conducted. No staff declined to take part in the study or objected in any way to being interviewed. All specialist areas of the work of the department in question were represented. Hourly-paid staff, although a significant group of staff within the department of the college, were excluded from the group. One of the key foreshadowed issues was the impact of new contracts of employment for full-time staff. This matter would have had little immediate relevance to hourly-paid staff. An additional reason for excluding such staff was the need to keep the respondents to a manageable number.

The final interview group was comprised as follows:

- All were lecturers in the creative arts department of the case study college
- All were on permanent full-time contracts
- They represented the full spread of curriculum specialism across the department
- All were either on the main lecturer or senior lecturer grade
- At the time of interview, all had between one and four years' experience as FE lecturers.

Thus the lecturers were all relatively new to teaching in FE, although some of them had other teaching experience. For reasons of confidentiality it is not possible to present detailed background information on the respondents. Although this prevents the reader fully contextualising either their comments or the analysis of the interview data, this consideration must be weighed against the guarantee given to the lecturers that their identities would not be revealed.

The decision on the number of respondents was largely dictated by two factors:

1. The need to limit the length and scope of the study to a reasonable and workable size given the timescale involved.
2. The need to take into account the detailed analysis to be carried out on the qualitative interview data.

The first point refers to a common factor in all small-scale case studies which neither have the advantage of external funding nor additional research staff. The second point is perhaps of more considerable significance. It is an advantage of open-ended qualitative interviews that the data which they produce can be analysed at considerable depth. In order to draw out shades of meaning and interpretations, it appeared sensible to limit the group size to allow adequate coverage of the full range and implications of the respondents' statements and their significance for FE policy and practice.

The methodology of data analysis

Glaser and Strauss's (1967) constant comparative method was employed for data analysis. This is an inductive form of data analysis in which the generation of theory is a continually developing process. Tentative categories are generated from the data and subsequent data are used to 'test' the validity of those categories. This method is consistent both with the identification of foreshadowed problems and the progressive focusing that is built into the research design.

Accordingly, it was felt appropriate to model the analysis of the qualitative interviews upon a five-stage procedure proposed by McCracken (1988) which incorporated the above strategies: each interview was carefully read through many times in order to reach an initial awareness and understanding of the key issues and problems it revealed. An attempt was made to adhere to two important principles. The first principle is that during the first stage of analysis, individual statements are to be judged for 'intensive' meaning, that is, with little concern for their larger significance. An attempt was made to pay little attention to the supposed importance of the data to the research problem. Issues identified within each transcript were initially simply listed, without regard to frequency of occurrence or how important or trivial they seemed. The aim during the first stage of data analysis was to avoid unconsciously imposing preconceived understandings and assumptions upon the data (Rowan 1981).

It was intended to delay, until the second stage of analysis, application of the ideas and concepts explored in the literature review to the interview data. During both the first and second stages, each interview was analysed as a unique project and considered in isolation from the other interviews. The experience of making a genuine attempt to adhere to these two principles was interesting. It is true to say that maintaining an open stance towards the data, (Glaser and Strauss 1965), thus avoiding premature closure, whilst applying concepts generated from

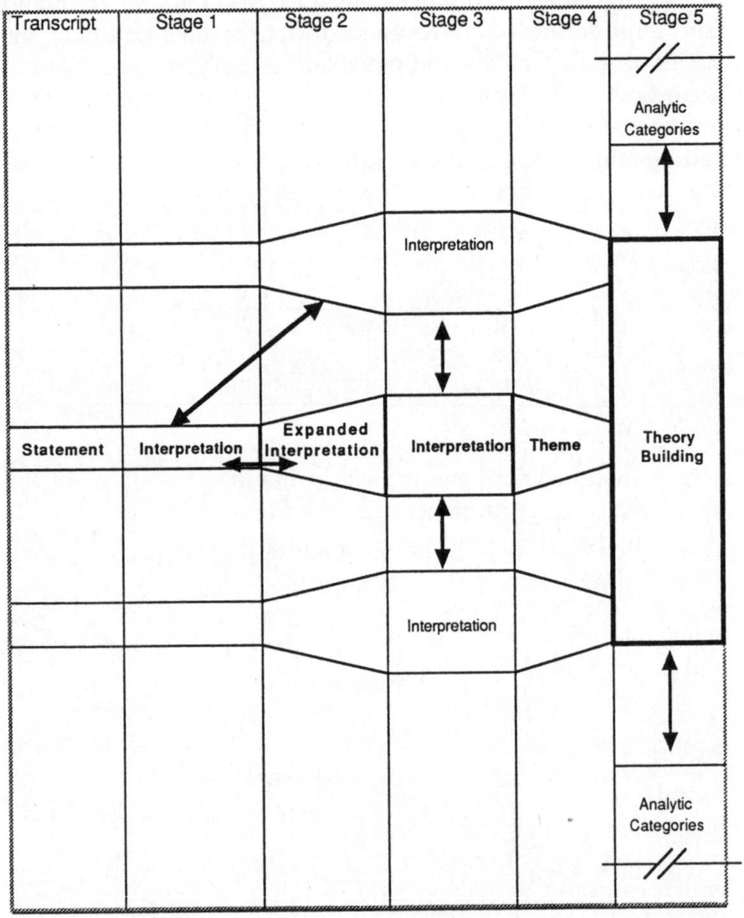

Figure 3.1 The long qualitative interview: stages of analysis (Adapted from McCracken 1988, p.43)

the review of the literature appears to pull in opposite directions. It would be fairer to say that a creative tension is maintained, where the focus shifts between the intrinsic meaning of the data and the extrinsic meanings and interpretations generated from the literature, personal experience and other influences. At best, an awareness of the problem of meaning imposition is achieved, and a genuine attempt to avoid it is made. A significant amount of looping back did occur between Stages One and Two, and between interviews, however, and McCracken's model of the stages of analysis of the long qualitative interview was adapted accordingly (see Figure 3.1). The second stage of analysis thus involved developing the ideas which arose from the first stage, sorting and grouping those with a common focus, and expanding their implications. The more general interpretations generated were then related back to the whole transcript of the interview. As noted above, however, separating stage one and stage two was not always possible – nor, it can be argued, was it consistent with a developing and emergent analytical process.

In the third stage, analyses of each interview were compared, in order to develop further interpretations of a more general nature.

The fourth stage involved making judgements as to the emergent themes which were implicit in the interpretations of the interviews. A large number of sub-themes were identified at this stage, but they were gradually subsumed within a smaller number, which can be termed 'meta-themes'.

The final stage was a review and comparison of meta-themes across interviews, with the aim of generating analytic categories, and theory building.

Since the formatted interview transcripts comprised over 300 pages, it was appropriate to use a simple data string search capability within the word processing software used. The edit command 'Find/Change' locates any occurrence of a user-defined word, partial word, or phrase. This facility was not, it must be stressed, used as an alternative to the immersion in the data which can only be gained from reading transcripts, research notes, and so on. Rather, its value was to check that *all* occurrences of a particular word or phrase were considered, and to aid data sorting, categorising and frequency counts.

Limitations of the study

The limitations of this study fall into three linked areas: theory, methodology, and generalisability.

Theory

The dearth of research on the relationship of theory to policy and practice at all levels in the FE sector generally has benefits and drawbacks. For example, a difficulty was that the study had to move beyond its immediate focus in order to demonstrate linkages to existing theoretical constructs, and it needed to draw upon a broad educational literature where theoretical work on the basis of teachers' practice is located. On the other hand, there was the advantage of originality, in that for the same reasons the study would be breaking new ground by looking specifically at FE lecturers' articulated perspectives upon their practice and related policy issues.

The point was made earlier that not all foreshadowed problems proved to be significant to respondents and that some others took on a greater significance than was anticipated. Whilst this offered a rich source of ideas which informed the study, a developing and emergent theoretical orientation was not without its difficulties for the researcher. One consequence and disadvantage of the grounded and tiered approach to data collection and analysis described in this chapter is that as the focus of the study shifts, even if only to a small degree, then some theorising becomes less central and other, hitherto excluded, theory becomes more so. Thus the literature cited cannot be said to be definitive of the theoretical orientation but evolved as the study progressed, with changes and adaptations being made during both the data collection and data analysis phases. Rather than seen as a limitation, this process should be highlighted as a positive aspect of qualitative research methodologies, which are thus able to take account of changing circumstances in the field and the interaction between theory, methods and analysis.

Methodology

The methodology for the study drew heavily upon the role of the participant observer and the technique of the qualitative interview. An important criticism of participant observation is that the research site can be over-familiar to the investigator, so that familiar routines are taken for granted (Becker 1971, p.10) with the result that events which are commonplace to a participant are overlooked and their significance can be lost (Measor and Woods 1991, p.70). The literature on participant observation methodology is helpful here. It points to the need for the researcher who employs this method to maintain an anthropological strangeness to the situation (Erikson 1986, p.121), a sense of 'critical enquiry' (Adler 1993, p.161). The writer used the guidelines given by Burgess (1984) in an attempt to overcome the problem:

> First, researchers should continually pose questions about the settings within which they are located. Secondly, researchers should write down in as much detail as possible what they have observed. Thirdly, observation should be regularly reviewed and cross-referenced to other activities and events that have been observed so that themes can be developed and in turn linked with the theoretical perspective that is deployed within the research project. (p.28)

An important factor in deciding to carry out open-ended interviews was that they enabled the writer to capitalise upon a technique advocated by Burgess, that of deliberately asking naïve questions to explore the taken-for-granted meanings held by respondents. Through reviewing the literature on participant research, a strategy was formulated which involved developing a style and form of questioning which at once distanced the researcher from the familiarity of the setting, and at the same time encouraged respondents to describe and analyse their taken-for-granted experience.

The qualitative interview is a well-established technique with a strong sociological tradition which supports its use (Whyte 1943; Becker et al. 1961; Glaser and Strauss 1967). The substantive focus of this research was upon lecturers' accounts: the recording of lecturers' perspectives, their reflections on their practice and upon related policy, and policy implementation in the corporate institution. As Bogdan and Biklen (1992) note, whether termed 'unstructured', 'open-ended', 'nondirective' or 'flexibly structured', the in-depth interview can be used by 'the researcher (who is) bent on understanding, in considerable detail, how people such as teachers, principals, and students think

and how they came to develop the perspectives they hold' (p.2).
Provided that appropriate questions are asked, and respondents
are prepared to provide the answers, a study of lecturers' accounts can illuminate important aspects of practice. It is part of
the writer's challenge to existing research on FE that lecturers'
accounts of their practice are seldom taken seriously as a basis
for theoretical analysis. Hammersley and Atkinson (1983), in
their primer on ethnography, emphasised this point: 'We can use
the accounts given by people as evidence of the perspectives of
particular groups or categories of actor to which they belong.
Indeed, knowledge of these perspectives may form an important element of the theory being developed' (p.106).

They also suggest that the ethnographic interview has dis-
tinct advantages over observations of behaviour in natural settings:

> To the extent that the aim in ethnography is not simply the
> provision of a description of what occurred in a particular
> setting over a certain period of time, there may be positive
> advantages to be gained from subjecting people to verbal
> stimuli different from those prevalent in the settings in
> which they normally operate. In other words, the 'artificial-
> ity' of the interview when compared with 'normal' events in
> the setting may allow us to understand how participants
> would behave in other circumstances, for example when
> they move out of a setting or when the setting changes.
> (p.119)

The key point here is that the advocacy in this study of the
reflective practitioner model made it essential that lecturers'
views were accessed, since they are central to the elaboration of
the model itself, and to understanding lecturers' own construc-
tions of reality. Lecturers' views, and the meanings which they
attach to their educational experiences, would be more difficult
to acquire using alternative methods.

Generalisability

It is important to be clear and unequivocal regarding the generalisability of the study, that is, the extent to which the findings
of the interviews used in this study can be generalised outside
of the case study college, or even within the college itself between different departments. The decision to interview a small

number of lecturers, all within the creative arts, brought with it the obligation to forego any claim to population validity or what Stenhouse calls 'predictive generalisability' (Stenhouse 1978, p.22). This is readily acknowledged, since all research designs carry with them both advantages and drawbacks, and it was felt that limiting the lecturer group, in this case to seven, brought with it clear compensating benefits in terms of the depth of data more readily available to the 'full participant' (Wagner 1993), representativeness within one curriculum area, and manageability. There was also the significant advantage that those lecturers in the group who had worked elsewhere shared a common experience of involvement in creative arts organisations, which provided useful insights into possible influences upon their approach to teaching and management.

It would have been unrealistic, given the resources at the writer's disposal, to have interviewed a large number of respondents and to have attempted in-depth qualitative analysis of the resulting data. The methodology was chosen for its potential in generating theory located in further education, through exploration of an instance of the policy, management and practice of teaching and learning processes in the FE sector.

It is a problem for qualitative research, such as that reported in this study, that in dealing with relatively small numbers of respondents, expressions of quantity such as 'many', 'most' and 'some' force the commonly understood meaning of these terms. It is nonetheless important to give the reader an indication of how common – or uncommon – certain responses were, within the strictly defined boundary of the lecturer group. At the same time, it is inappropriate to quantify responses in the majority of cases, except where a particular view was held by one lecturer or by all lecturers in the group. This is because to do so would give an unwanted and misleading quantitative dimension to qualitative data, and encourage potentially unhelpful statistical interpretations.

Given the above caveats, it is nonetheless possible to attach to this study a notion of generalisability which is different in kind from predictive generalisability – which is dependent upon statistical sampling techniques not employed in this study. The alternative notion of generalisability is what Stenhouse (1978, p.22) terms 'retrospective generalisability', which rests upon an individual respondent or a whole study being regarded as an instance rather than a sample. He identifies an important distinction between predictive and retrospective generalisation in relation to case study methodology. He makes the point that:

> ...the basis of verification and cumulation in the study of cases is the recognition that a case is an instance, though not, like a sample, a representative, of a class and that case study is a basis for generalisation and hence cumulation of data embedded in time. It is the classic instrument of analytic as opposed to narrative history. (p.21)

The case record based upon the field data of this study is one systematic way of mapping participants' experience. Making the record available to other researchers can achieve the aim of 'creating a critical and analytic contemporary history of education fed by recent, current and future case study' (p.22).

Other interpretations of this model of generalisation are sometimes referred to as 'relatedness', 'comparability' or 'recognisability'; these variants share the idea that if qualitative research is disseminated to the participants, or to others who have experience of the setting within which the research has been based, it should read 'as it feels to be in it' (p.34). The implication of this is that if this study rings true to those within in the case study college, and more broadly within the FE sector, then the benefits of generalisability may attach to the study, even though statistically speaking the appropriate caveats, as described above, would of course apply. As Stenhouse puts it: 'Retrospective generalisations are attempts to map the range of experience rather than to perceive within that range the operation of laws in the scientific sense' (p.22). It is entirely appropriate, within the context of a small-scale study, to contribute to such a mapping exercise, within the constraints and limitations identified within this chapter.

Acknowledged limitations can also have positive aspects. As a lone researcher it was important, as hinted above, to recognise the restrictions of time and resources which accompany the role. It is the responsibility of the researcher to ensure that the methods employed are not only appropriate to the subject and context of the research, but are also manageable and within the resources available to the individual.

Balancing scope and coverage with involvement as a partici- pant has, it is argued, strengthened the study by stimulating a productive interaction between practitioner insight, theoretical orientation, and the application of a focused research method- ology. Small-scale educational case studies, carried out by prac- titioners and other researchers in the workplace, can be used as the basis for comparative studies across and between educa- tional sectors. In this way, it is possible to argue that ecological validity can be established through a comparative survey of individually separate, but theoretically or substantively related, cases.

The credibility of educational research for the teachers and administrators on whom it is often focused and to whom it is often addressed may depend wholly upon how recognisable are the resultant descriptions and concepts to those groups. It is one outcome of the progressive focusing which both structured the data collection, and provided an emergent theoretical frame- work, that the next three chapters are organised around themes which became clearly evident during the conversations, inter- views and reflections which took place during the active data gathering phase in the college.

The emergent model of lecturer practice is presented as both grounded in the reported perspectives of FE lecturers upon their work, and inspired by, and consistent with an important theo- retical tradition of critical pedagogy. It is suggested that the qualitative methods employed in this study contributed in a major way to its theoretical outcomes. Careful attention to fore- shadowed problems based upon prior knowledge, experience and reflection upon practice, willingness to adopt an open re- search technique in order fully to explore issues reported as significant by participants, and a commitment to an emergent theoretical framework informed by progressive focusing, it is argued are appropriate and powerful methodological proce- dures within the study.

The ensuing three chapters detail the results and findings of the case study, linking these to the national and institutional context of the incorporation of the FE sector.

CHAPTER FOUR

Quality Assurance

This chapter focuses upon some of the effects of the incorporation of the FE sector. The responses of the lecturer group to the
idea of a market in education are given, and the issue of quality
assurance is examined in detail. Alternative notions of quality
assurance in use by the lecturers, and which focus upon classroom interaction, are explored.

Cultural-political change in further education

The cultural-political ethos of colleges of further education has
shifted markedly in the last two years. Recent legislation affecting the FE sector, allied to major reorganisation of the vocational
curriculum and new funding arrangements have combined to
destabilise college organisation. Governing bodies are now
comprised of a majority of business representatives, the funding
for non-vocational courses has collapsed and decision-making
takes place within a tight financial framework set by a central-
ised funding council and implemented by college accountants
and finance directors.

   The implication that central government policy for education
was out of sympathy with the concerns of educational practice
led one lecturer to argue that government is imposing an economic paradigm upon education: '…under the current climate,
there are so many aspects of education that are being pushed
down from central government, from a distance, from people
whose contact with practical education is minimal.'

   One of the dangers inherent in the emerging view of colleges
as businesses was foreshadowed by another lecturer:

...the college as it stands at the moment is a business, or we've been told it's a business and if it is a business then, if we see it in those terms, then this business is going to go down the pan because you always have a head team of management who knows who their customers are, what their customers want...and this company doesn't know...

There was evidence to suggest a concern that the desire by government to move colleges towards a business orientation, and to subject them to increased competition within an educational market, had taken place without adequate preparation and ground laying at the college level. One lecturer, for example, liked the idea of colleges as 'autonomous organisations who offer something and attract students to it', but insisted that the policy has been undermined by the lack of adequate development support for college managers.

Another noted that the imposition of policy-driven changes upon colleges may have brought with it a lack of ownership of external initiatives on the part of educational managers, making the important point that by this strategy 'you're encouraged to have a negative attitude, even by the people who are presenting it'.

For most lecturers, incorporation has simply not delivered what had been promised. The following view was typical:

Well I have to say I've found it very difficult to see any tangible benefits in terms of the kind of promised land that was held out to us when the discussions originally took place. In terms of funding I've not seen any huge benefit, I mean there was a great deal of talk about there not being sticky fingers from the local authority or whatever, most of the monetary advantages that were perceived to exist don't seem to have turned into anything you can touch, feel or use, so I mean at the chalk face or whatever I can't see that there has been a huge benefit.

The idea of competition, and the introduction of an increasingly competitive ethos following incorporation, emerged as a strong issue of concern to the lecturers in the study. They feel under pressure from college managers to make efficiency gains, for example by employing more part-time staff who came cheaper than full-timers, in order to become more competitive. Staffing and equipment budgets are continually being reviewed and trimmed, and an internal bidding system has been introduced for capital expenditure. This competitive ethos is regarded by lecturers with caution. Most lecturers dislike the idea of the college being placed in competition with schools, and have even greater reservations about internal competition. As one put it: 'One has become very aware within the college that there is a cake and you're competing for the slices of it; competing for the bigger slices, that's obviously out of one's hands.' Competition has a clear effect upon staff's relationships with each other, and promotes 'challenges about resources and about which area's more important'.

There are negative consequences in business terms of introducing a competitive market in education. Staff are worried about practical issues like the loss of economies of scale and the prospect of a smaller pool of resources, as well as broader concerns to do with lack of accountability, the inadequacies of college management in terms of their business acumen and the extent to which college managers are under-prepared to deal with incorporation.

Many lecturing staff perceived that there will be a period of uncertainty and entrenchment for college management, whilst they get used to their new responsibilities and powers under incorporation. This theme of uncertainty reappears in most lecturers' accounts of the impact of incorporation. The impression of one lecturer is both incisive and typical:

> Initially I see that management will still be scrabbling about trying to establish their own identity rather than having the cushion of a local authority; they'll try and establish their own identity so they might tread on a few people while that's happening. The lecturing staff, I think, won't be taken into account for the next 18 months, 2 years. Perhaps after that, once they achieved a suitable balance, they might start consulting again.

The introduction of a business efficiency model of education was declared by nearly all lecturers in the study to be undesirable. Reducing costs of the sector was seen by one lecturer as part of a deliberate government objective to bring 'downward pressure on funding (in) the long term'. For another lecturer, the impact of increased enrolments upon the employment totals and a shift in emphasis from education to employment training, has turned FE into 'not so much a dumping ground, but a way of off-loading certain kinds of problems about training and education'.

The model of education was recognised by most lecturers to operate across sectors:

> Well, I mean the great opting out schools thing seems to be the land of milk and honey...and a number of schools have drifted headlong into that, and taken it up with some enthusiasm, and time will tell whether or not they are best served. I think there is generally a movement towards wanting to teach more people more cheaply, and this is true in HE...

Most lecturers rejected in strong terms the notion of applying a business model to education, which might be considered surprising, given the assumed business orientation of the sector as a whole: 'I hate it! I hate the idea! It's what sort of college plc is, it's forcing the college even more, it's forcing colleges to operate as businesses. They shouldn't be, they should be subsidised to a huge degree.'

There was a strong sense of blame attached to the government which introduced reforms without adequately preparing those whose task it would be to implement them. In the view of one lecturer, the creation of a newly independent FE sector and the government expectation that college managers should somehow be equipped to deal with the new circumstance in which they find themselves, is flawed: 'I think a lot of the problems are stemming from their ignorance, and I don't use that as a negative – that's a point of fact – they are ignorant about how to operate in that sector.'

The removal of responsibility for education from the state into private hands strikes against a strongly-held ideological position of most lecturers. The strength of feeling on this issue, signified in the ensuing extract, was expressed during the interview cycle by almost all lecturers in the study:

> Education should be the responsibility of government or the state, I suppose (by the state I mean us as a democratic state) – it is within that province, it shouldn't be a private enterprise. The idea of it being a private enterprise is anathema to me, and that's the way it's moving at the moment...the sense that the resources that a student can count on are dependent on the business efficiency, and the competitive business

efficiency, of an educational organisation is appalling. It makes me angry – I get inarticulate about it because I get so angry.

Another lecturer argued that the direction of government policy for the FE sector is towards an inferior two-tier education system, which ties quality to ability to pay and consequently brings about social inequality:

> ...I am generally very concerned, and worried if you like, that we are going for cheap, mass education. And that we're moving to a society where, if you can pay for it, you will get quality, and if you can't you will get a basic, competence based training if you like, and therefore the gap, if you like, the social gaps, they're going to widen...

A strong thread which links most lecturers' accounts of the impact of the market upon education is the recognition of political influences. Many lecturers recognised that the government's educational policy of centralisation of power and decentralisation of responsibility is part of a wider policy direction towards public sector services and organisations as a whole:

> ...I just do not believe that the values of the market, the market place can be simply dropped, imposed upon the public services, the professional services, the services to people, education, health, whatever – I think it will lead to disaster, I think there is evidence coming out of the health service now that it has lead to disaster, the kind of disaster that it will lead to in education will obviously be different to that, but will be equally serious I think.

The speed and scope of change is unprecedented. Lecturers have experienced acute loss of control of their work situation. This phenomenon has also been noted with regard to school teachers (Ball 1993a). There is a real tension in colleges between the management-imposed imperatives of satisfying quantitative performance indicators, and lecturers' conceptions and priorities based upon their value judgements. The result of squeezing resources, vocationalisation of the curriculum, and increasing external accountability, is that lecturers are forced to engage in trading-off learners' needs, course needs, and their former ideas about practices which count as teaching. In many cases, lecturers' biographies have been built around a conception of teaching which would deny the very market model they are required to implement. There is a climate of suspicion in colleges, which fosters distrust of initiatives such as flexible learning and work-based assessment. The fear is that such developments are purportedly introduced to serve students' needs but will be used by unscrupulous managers to further undermine lecturers' ownership of legitimate work.

The dominance of the notion of quality assurance

Quality is a slippery notion and this is reflected in common usage where there is frequently slippage between its use as an adjective (= quality as a relative concept) and as a noun (= quality as an absolute concept). Quality assurance is a powerful concept which permeates the ethos and operation of post-compulsory education today (Elliott 1993). It has replaced 'responsiveness to clients' needs' and 'market awareness' as the *sine qua non* of the sector.

As argued elsewhere:

> There is an everyday sense in which the term has long been applied to educational processes and outcomes. In the political arena of recent years, however, the term has been inseparably linked to notions of efficiency and cost effectiveness, which have their origin in the 'Great Debate' concerning educational standards and costs, launched following Callaghan's Ruskin College speech in October 1976. (Elliott 1993, p.34)

Student feedback, peer review and self-assessment have been key components of the course review and evaluation process within post-compulsory education, focused upon improvement of quality. Quality assurance, as a topic of some importance to the lecturers, emerged during a very early stage of the fieldwork. Many lecturers regard as problematic some prevailing definitions and interpretations of quality that are held by college managers. Similarly, they are sceptical towards the imposition and implementation within FE colleges of quality assurance systems derived from industry, and thus designed outside the educational context.

Sallis (1992) argues that the upsurge in interest in quality in education coincided with the ERA (DES 1988a), which placed considerable emphasis on measuring 'outputs' from colleges.

However, the ERA did not appear in a vacuum. FE had already seen the introduction of the staff-student ratio by the Audit Commission in the early 1980s as an important measure of college efficiency. 1987 saw the publication of the seminal DES report 'Managing Colleges Efficiently' (DES 1987), and many of its policy points fed directly into the 1988 ERA legislation. The recommendations of the ERA on FE were embodied in Circular 9/88 (DES 1988b), which proposed a radical agenda for colleges which included applying performance indicators, most notably the staff-student ratio, to assess college efficiency, and the application of unit-costing as an efficiency factor.

Socio-political factors are most significant, and here the adoption of a comparative perspective between FE and HE is fruitful. The ERA also established the Polytechnic and Colleges Funding Council, which took responsibility for the funding of non-university HE institutions away from local authorities and gave it to a new quango, which from the start signalled its intention to improve efficiency in the HE sector. As Maclure (1992) notes:

> The Government believed that if strategic decisions about the planning of courses and the allocation of resources were taken nationally, each college could then be allowed to stand on its own two feet with its own autonomous board of governors. The governors and the senior academic staff would then be encouraged to act like entrepreneurs, managing their college in response to the policy signals and cash incentives emanating from the funding council and from local industry. There would be no role in this for the local authorities. (p.99)

This same model, presumably for the same reasons, was applied to the FE sector four years later, when the FHE Act (DES 1992) set up the FEFC and took the 'free market' view of educational institutions to its logical conclusion by giving FE colleges corporate status. Direct comparisons between the government's intentions for the FE and HE sectors with respect to funding, control and political direction became even easier to draw after the appointment of the Director of the PCFC (Bill Stubbs), who had led that body through its formative period, as Director of the FEFC. In many respects the FEFC has mirrored the PCFC in its policies, including the imposition of a 'clawback' of funding if colleges fail to meet funding targets or persuade staff to sign new contracts, the introduction of a competitive bidding system for growth in student numbers, and space efficiency measures.

The quality movement in FE can be seen as part of a government-inspired steer towards increased efficiency in education. Parallel trends exist in the schools sector – fuelling the continuing 'opting out' debate – and the model is being applied in the health service through the imposition of a quasi-market among competing cost centres, and in local authorities through the privatisation of certain amenities and the introduction of compulsory competitive tendering.

Whose quality is it anyway?

A key determining characteristic of quality assurance systems in education is seen to be the clear preference expressed for quality systems imported from industry (FEU 1991: 3). What does this tell us about the model of education which is being employed? Can a quality system designed for manufacturing industries be applied to education? What is the 'product' of an educational system/institution? Most colleges engaged in the implementation of BS 5750 define their product or output as 'the student learning experience'. However, it is then necessary for them to go on to explain what is, and therefore what is not, student learning. BS 5750 works by using a system of document control. The system is based upon documented procedures, specified in advance by the institution, and which are nominated as relating to the specified output. Only those procedures deemed by the BS registered institution to be 'within document control' are taken into account. It is not, therefore, difficult to imagine why the use of such a procedure has been attacked as reductionist when it is applied to the teaching and learning process.

It is also interesting to note in passing that many advocates of the introduction of formal quality systems into educational institutions themselves freely acknowledge the dissonance between such institutions and the industrial/commercial sector within which such quality systems were developed. For example: 'It would be inappropriate and foolish to propose that what worked for Japanese industry is appropriate for British industry let alone British schools' (West-Burnham 1992, p.14).

The same point is made by the FEFC (1993a) in their *Quality Assessment Circular 93/28*:

> The education service can learn from the approaches to quality and its assurance adopted in the business and industry sectors. However, the different aims and objectives of a public service, which take account of the needs of the community as a whole as well as those of individual consumers, must be reflected in its quality assurance arrangements. (p.7)

An important distinction to bear in mind when thinking about quality systems is: are they about doing the right thing, or are they about doing the thing right? It is around what the 'right thing' is that educationalists tend to choose their battleground, yet it is possible to concede that there may be many different ways to achieve the same aims. Educational administrators and managers, on the other hand, may be more concerned with systems – in other words, with doing the thing right. Does this point to an explanation of the growing popularity of quality assurance, given the FEFC push towards increasing student numbers in the sector whilst reducing the unit of resource?

Sallis (1992) wishes to make a distinction between BS 5750, as a quality assurance system which 'focuses on the quality of an organisation's systems' (p.106), and Total Quality Management (TQM) which, he suggests, is more about 'quality as an all-embracing holistic concept' (p.106). He describes the TQM approach as based upon the customer – supplier chain, the idea that everybody is the supplier and customer of everybody else. He suggests that acceptance by colleges of this concept will turn the organisational hierarchy upside down – that is, the manager's role shifts from directing staff to supporting staff. He claims that this is not an abrogation of management responsibility but a recognition of management's duty to embrace the principle of customer/demand-led culture. In structural terms, it is cross-college organisational teams which deliver the 'quality service' to the 'customer'.

There does, however, seem in practice to be more in common between these systems than divides them. Whether or not the perceived focus of TQM is upon changing the culture of a college, the rhetoric is that of the market. Ball (1993b) has described the ways in which market ideology has permeated government educational policy; such an ideology has also been perceived to operate at the level of organisational policy within the FE sector (Elliott and Hall 1994). Thus, institutional autonomy is challenged both through the centralising tendency of central government policy towards FE and also through the increasingly widespread adoption and imposition of human resource management policies and procedures for lecturing staff.

Lecturers' perspectives on quality

A foreshadowed problem which informs the study is that a drawback of industry-derived initiatives in education seems to be the inappropriateness for their intended use, which in part appears to derive from an over-reliance upon quantitative data at the expense of the qualitative (Elliott and Crossley 1994). In order to investigate the nature of the performance and efficiency measures in place, the lecturers in this study were asked a range of questions on human resource management, outcome-based staff development and qualifications, the impact of the market in education, performance indicators, and other quality assurance systems and procedures in use in the college. At the time of the study, the college was preparing to be audited in preparation for its application for BS5750 accreditation.

Lecturers' responses indicate that it is the language and insensitive application of formal quality assurance systems more than the procedures themselves that are often the main focus of criticism. One lecturer acknowledged the need for a formal approach to quality assurance:

> I do think there is a need in terms of quality, I do think there is a need for us, I think we are all aware of it, I am anyway, there has been, for quite some time, a need for us to formalise more the way in which we record and monitor what we do...that is only a process of formalising something that in a sense already either exists or ought to exist.

The most inexperienced lecturer in the interview group found some aspects of the BS5750 system in use valuable: 'Some of the procedures which I found in the book are quite good, whether that's just a college-based thing or the principle of BS5750 I don't know. Some forms and procedures laid out in there seem to be very helpful.'

There are, however, a range of views weighted against the mechanistic model which underpins the BS5750 system. One lecturer insisted that kitemark quality systems embody an external and inappropriate value-system based upon the market, making the point that fundamental assumptions 'about what is the product of education, who the customer is in education, and so on...', remain unaddressed. Another joked that 5750 is 'just a number that comes out of a bingo hall. My experience of it so far is not at all positive...it's just a number of a job just to fill somebody's post'. It was pointed out by another lecturer that kitemark quality assurance systems are not only inappropriate models for use in education but are also going out of fashion in industry and commerce.

Whilst senior managers recognised that staff had objections to the use of BS5750, they failed to recognise the critical problem with BS5750: that it puts in place a technicistic and bureaucratic approach to organisational procedures, and that it is non-evaluative: 'To overcome some of the philosophical difficulties which staff have expressed with BS5750, it is being written with the curriculum as the major focus. This ensures that the quality of the students' learning experience is our central concern, rather than the bureaucracy which is customary with BS5750' (College Newsletter).

Focusing quality assurance upon 'the quality of the students' learning experience' (College Newsletter) was an objective shared by all of the lecturers in this study. However, contrary to the declared intention, the implementation of BS5750 in the college is immensely bureaucratic, and dozens of forms are issued as part of the 5750 quality manual.

This theme was picked up by several lecturers in this study who articulated an alternative approach to quality assurance which draws upon notions of individuals and teams reflecting and reviewing. One lecturer considered that performance indicators should be internalised by staff: '...performance indicators – you shouldn't have to be told to do that, you should be working at that yourself anyway within the institution.' Another agreed that 'I think that it's up to us to set our performance indicators – if you like'. A contrasting view was offered by this lecturer, who had concerns about the veracity of internal performance indicators:

There are too many temptations with internal assessment of performance indicators I think. Whether or not you necessarily agree with what those performance indicators are, if they are being externally assessed then you do feel that they are being assessed on some sort of rational and fair basis.

An interesting conclusion drawn by one lecturer, observing the impact which quality assurance systems have in education, is that education has itself been to blame for allowing a vacuum to form which was rapidly filled by 'mechanistic approaches' once it became necessary for quality assurance systems to be put into place in order to secure continuation of funding.

One lecturer's view was that this process would do nothing to improve the quality of the student experience:

I believe in appraisal, I believe in lecturers and any professionals being involved in appraisals, but that's not the same as having a kite mark, I mean do you get a stamp on your bottom?... Again it's quantitative rather than qualitative isn't it, it's all to do with numbers, to do with how many people are achieving at such and such a level, and that will obviously affect how much...it will affect your resources or in fact whether you exist as an institution or not. The problem with any kind of those statistics is that they don't tell the whole story or they can tell whatever part of the story...they appear to be objective but they are subject to subjective interpretation.

Another lecturer pointed out that kitemark quality assurance systems are not only inappropriate models for use in education, but are also going out of fashion in industry and commerce:

I hear from my colleagues who are working in business that (quality systems are) old news and I fear that yet again we're getting into a situation that will be five years out of date and we'll be doing things lagging behind what is thought to be good practice and it has always happened and the reason is, of course, that people are trying to graft on to education, which is a different beast, models that are inappropriate for it. As long as people try to do that there will be no change...

This lecturer voiced a common view that any acceptable alternative system must embody characteristics which are grounded in the working practices of those for whom it is designed:

> We're all aware from Brecht that if you're gonna actually go for making changes in society you do it a way that addresses the audience. So we're constantly checking what we're doing, or our ideas against a criteria, that of either a group of people who are called critics, who have some sort of specialist knowledge or bums on seats. So I've never had a problem with that. I think it is very sad, in a sense, that a system hasn't been designed that enables my performance as a lecturer to be judged by my students' performance. If my A Level results this year are terrible, which I'm afraid they might well be, that may reflect badly on my teaching, so that's clearly not a strategy, because I could have taught very well but have had a really bad group of students this year. So it has to be something else that says: 'yes you did everything OK, right, but it didn't work for these cases, how can we address that?'

Underpinning the suspicion with which kitemarked quality systems were regarded was the view, expressed by this lecturer, that they embody an external and inappropriate value system – that of the market:

> I just do not believe that the values of the market, the market place can be simply dropped, imposed upon the public services, the professional services, the services to people, education, health, whatever – I think it will lead to disaster, I think there is evidence coming out of the health service now that it *has* lead to disaster, the kind of disaster that it will lead to in education will obviously be different to that, but will be equally serious I think.

This lecturer went on to argue that the criteria of the appropriateness of quality assurance systems for education is a key consideration:

> And because that (i.e. BS 5750) is basically as I understand it, a commercial industry standard, the question that arises in my mind is how appropriate is it to what we deliver? And how much does that involve, if you like, assumptions being made without really being thought about, about what is the product of education, who the customer is in education and so on and it does seem to me that, almost overnight, we are starting to be encouraged to use a particular language to describe what we do which in a sense which has come, which

has simply been imported, lock, stock and barrel from the market sector, from the commercial sector.

In imposing kitemark quality assurance systems, many lecturers felt that college management were blurring the distinction between quality as a system and quality as a value, manifested as a commitment to resourcing measures to improve the quality of the student learning experience. As one lecturer put it:

> I'm never sure whose idea of quality is being assured or to what end it's being assured. I mean working here you couldn't help but be sceptical when you felt that there were all these moves in place to make sure we were given this badge of quality or whatever and yet there didn't appear to be much serious effort to put the resources in place to allow any quality of delivery to take place. And so quality became a word which was largely devoid of meaning. Again it depends whether it is something – an idea that means something or if it is just a means to an end, you have to have this thing in order to get FE funding so you have to qualify for it, or whether it carries with it a sense of responsibility and genuine meaning. Again I suppose the antagonism towards the college management generally has made a lot of people very sceptical… And it's indicative of peoples' general feelings I think towards what quality has meant to those people who make decisions in this college. I would like to be wrong, I suppose.

For the lecturers, focusing quality assurance on the quality of the students' learning experience is more to do with understanding everyday interactions between lecturing staff and students: '…it would seem to me that if they're to bring decision-making down to a lower level you'd be able to maintain quality and probably make savings if you make it in the interest of the people concerned with the actual curriculum delivery to save the money.' What is being suggested here is a re-examination of the locus of decision making for colleges as a strategy both to improve quality and save money.

A preferred approach to quality for many lecturers is one which which displays some of the characteristics of the reflective practitioner model (Schon 1983). A common theme emerging from the interview data is that lecturers do engage, as part of their everyday existing practice, in reflection upon their work, both individually and as members of course teams:

> We constantly sit around informally, in pairs or whatever, talking about how one can do things better. We have formal structures at team meetings where we're reflecting on our working practices, on the past, on the future, it happens then...when we talk a lot about operational procedures and things. But also there have been, and I've been there, when we've talked about the philosophy of things and how we're going about things and they're the most valuable and most enjoyable things that one does.

As another lecturer put it, 'we are constantly reflecting on what we're doing...' The frequent use of the 'we' form in lecturers' perspectives on quality reminds the writer of the centrality, for them, of a collegial approach:

> I mean I think we in the creative areas have a responsibility...to realise that if you're teaching hairdressing, presumably for example, from the top of the tongue as it were, you know, that involves the same kind of reflection, the same kind of approach, and that that's what in the end, hopefully should provide the quality for the students, is that we are constantly reflecting on what we're doing...

In the FE context, the notion of a collaborative course team repeatedly recurs as the unit which lecturers see as having the potential to guarantee the quality of the student experience. As one lecturer said:

> BTEC encourages it all the time, it encourages you to review your procedures, review as individuals the way you're doing things, what your aims are and review as a course – you have to submit a course review, which is great because it focuses your mind. They are doing that all the time, you're reflecting as an individual, as part of an informal unit and as part of a formal unit all time.

The introduction of BS 5750 as a quality standard in the case study college provides, for the lecturers in this study, a profound and indicative example of the promotion by college managers of an initiative rooted in a managerialist culture. A key determining characteristic of quality assurance systems in education has been recognised, by the FE sector's own research and development body, to be the clear preference expressed for quality systems imported from industry (FEU 1991, p.3). The require-ment that the college specified what it designated as its 'product' for the purposes of 'auditing' provides a clear signal to college managers to apply hard business methodology to their opera-tions, accelerates the process of commodification of the learning and teaching process, and encourages managers to draw a narrow and technicistic interpretation of the role and function of the college and its staff.

In the case study college it is almost impossible to engage with work on course monitoring, evaluation and review, or to attend a meeting with senior managers, without having to take account of BS 5750 procedures. The procedures define and modify what lecturers are authorised to do within the college and provide a measure by which lecturers' actions can be moni-tored and evaluated. Internal inspection of the system involves lecturers from outside the department acting as auditors by checking that documentation is in place and up to date.

The operation of BS5750 as a quality assurance system has little to do with the sense in which the lecturers in this study refer to the quality of the student learning experience. Whilst, as has been shown, they have no difficulty with formal assessment of quality, the use of performance indicators and the general notion of external accountability, it seems clear that around the notion of quality within the college there is a major ideological battleground. Within the managerialist culture, the term has been inseparably linked to notions of efficiency, accountability to a mechanistic and inappropriate standard and cost-effective-ness: all linked to college regulations and procedures rather than classroom practice. Government policy does not see any contra-diction between notions of efficiency or competition in educa-tion and quality of learning; on the contrary, it would argue that the operation of market forces gives students a better deal.

The key issue at the heart of the debate concerning the use of quality systems concerns the multiple understandings by stake-holders in the system about notions of autonomy and freedom. Certainly the lecturers in this study feel that managers are pressing to gain more control over the teaching and learning process following incorporation – what one lecturer calls 'the blanket approach' – and they are agreed that the proposed new conditions of service for lecturing staff are symptomatic of such a trend (Ward 1993).

In the case study college some staff feel obliged to implement many of the new systems, including BS 5750, in order not to cause difficulties for themselves and their students. As one lecturer put it:

> Where funding is according to outcome and the kind of funding that you're going to have for your course next year, and the kind of resources that you're going to be able to put into place next year, then there's clearly a conflict of interests because you don't want to be seen to be not achieving the required standard, you don't want students to fail if it's going to impede your ability to deliver to your next cohort of students.

However, a warning note for college managers is that compliance does not necessarily mean that innovations will be implemented in full (Joyce and Showers 1988), and it can breed mediocrity (Becher and Kogan 1992, p.180).

The hostility of most staff to managerialist culture finds its expression in what Firestone and Corbett (1988, p.324) call 'co-optation'. In one instance, a failure to take the pre-existing practices of the department into account in determining human resourcing policy leads to less efficient part-time staffing allocations being made. A policy which had served its purpose in other departments is applied without question to a department which was, in fact, operating a more efficient system. The combination of myth, division of management responsibility and uncritical application of numerical formula to dynamic practice is enough to undermine one of the key elements of the managerialist culture: that of the efficient and effective college. This works against the development of a sense of ownership of the managerialist culture (Miles 1987). The consequences of this are that the ability of senior managers to manage essential strategic functions is called into question and a negative-efficiency factor is built into everyday practice.

The policy of not empowering staff, but holding onto decision-taking roles, runs counter to Fullan's (1991) prescription for successful change processes, which are 'characterised by collaboration and close interaction among those central to carrying out the changes' (1991, p.349). This perspective was strongly endorsed by one lecturer, whose view is a typical one:

> I think that if the college wanted to find ways of saving money, which seems to be their one goal in life, then that could be done if the decisions were put in the hands of the people delivering the curriculum, because they would know what is achievable and what isn't...

There are a large number of 'bad' management decisions, variously described by lecturers in the study as heavy-handed, hierarchical and incompetent, which impact upon the day-to-day working practices of staff in an irksome and unpleasant manner. Resentment builds resistance, which serves to feed a counter-culture, sustained and supported by the activity of undermining initiatives which are designed to build a unified corporate culture.

For the lecturing staff in this study, it is where managerialism impacts and impinges upon the area of work which they regard as their central concern – the teaching and learning process – that most opposition occurred. What one lecturer described as 'almost an ivory tower mentality' amongst the college managers is recognised by all lecturers in the study. They are, without exception, appalled by the reductionist notion of education as a business, because business prioritises different values to education. One lecturer highlighted the different philosophical basis of managerialism: 'It is actually a change of philosophy from what is the most important thing is the student, the individual student, the individual pupil – what now appears, or what my perception of it is, is that the most important thing is an efficiently run organisation.'

Lecturers' opposition to managerialism expresses itself in a variety of ways, depending upon the nature of the perceived threat – does it threaten to impact upon valued practice or is it something that could be ignored or mocked? Where the threat is perceived as to be to the quality of teaching and learning, then lecturers respond with the resources at their disposal. Their response is not bloody-minded, nor is it without sympathy or understanding for the predicament in which college managers find themselves in having to implement government and FEFC policies. Sometimes the resistance is overt, where, for example, only one of the lecturers in the study complies with the requirement to keep the BS5750 manual up to date. In other cases, lecturers engage in what one called 'subversive, rather than overt, confrontation'; creative timetabling and *post hoc* completion of registers are common practices of this kind. However variable their responses are, and they differed in scope, type, and style, they are invariably grounded in an epistemological certainty as to the enduring value of lecturer-student interaction. This certainty is expressed through a firm belief in the lecturer's responsibility to meet the needs of the student, rather than institutional or systemic needs. As one lecturer put it: 'I think sometimes there is a kind of agenda for FE which serves the political needs of a particular government, or a set of ideas, rather than the educational needs of the people that it claims to serve.'

This view confirms the centrality, for lecturers themselves, of fully taking into account the orientations of the learner (Guy 1990, p.203). Underlying this belief is a recognition of the essential humanity of the student and the importance, for the development of the potential of the student, of the lecturer's influence, guidance and communication of knowledge and understanding. This commitment on the part of lecturers is often expressed practically in terms of 'trying to create a learning environment'.

Conclusion

The argument of this chapter is not intended to convey that quality systems are 'a bad thing' *per se*. It is, rather, that by virtue of their common origin and expression through a market ideology, they carry with them a powerful temptation for those who introduce them into educational institutions to impose a market model of quality which is, at bottom, reductionist, de-professionalising and contrary to the idea of education as a shared learning experience. In the market, quality becomes muddled with efficiency, and quality as a system becomes muddled with quality as a value. It should, in theory, be possible to embrace both ends of these continua, but it appears to defeat most who try. And perhaps to expect that it is possible to sustain the quality of the student experience, however defined, within managerialist quality systems, is both politically and pedagogically naïve.

CHAPTER FIVE

The Competent Lecturer

This chapter provides an overview of the development of the NCVQ framework, and looks in particular at the responses of the lecturers in the study to the TDLB NVQ Assessor Units, which were a requirement for those working with NVQ and GNVQ candidates. The philosophical basis of NVQs as competence-based qualifications is highlighted, and the limitations of their use as a training and development tool for lecturers are suggested.

Competence-based qualifications

In April 1985, the Government set up a working group – the Review of Vocational Qualifications (RVQ) – to review the whole range of vocational qualifications in England and Wales and 'to recommend a structure which was relevant, comprehensive and accessible, which recognised competence and was cost effective' (Deville 1987, p.10). The key outcomes of the working group were the setting up of the NCVQ to address the lack of coherence which was widely felt to characterise vocational education and training, and the recommendation of the development of an NVQ framework, designed and implemented by the NCVQ. Existing vocational qualifications offered by the then Business and Technician Education Council (BTEC) and other awarding bodies would, if satisfactory to NCVQ, be brought under the umbrella of the new national framework. The working group went further, and specified the character of the new qualifications:

> ...the review group felt strongly that vocational qualifications had to be first and foremost statements of competence

which took account not only of skills and knowledge but of the ability to apply these in a working situation. The group therefore recommended that the new National Council should provide for the specification of standards of competence which would be reflected in vocational qualifications brought within the NVQ framework. (Deville 1987, p.11)

Two key principles of the NCVQ framework are made clear, then, from the outset. The qualification is to be competence-based and competences are to be demonstrated in the workplace. These two principles hold for the full range of qualifications which fall within the NCVQ framework. The requirement that the framework is a comprehensive one means that it is intended eventually to encompass all occupations at all levels from school-leaver trainee to manager. NVQs currently cover some 80 per cent of the working population and extend across all major sectors of employment.

In taking on board the principle that vocational qualifications are to be consequent upon assessment in the workplace, NCVQ was drawing upon the structure already in use by the Training Agency – which adopted a competence-based assessment model established in Youth Training Scheme training, aimed at low-level occupations. The model has, however, also been widely used for management training and development, and adopted by the industry lead body, the Management Charter Initiative, and the National Forum for Management Education and Development. NCVQ levels now range from 1 (basic/un-skilled/trainee) to 5 (advanced/professional/managerial).

Industry lead body standards in FE

Lecturers in this study saw the impact of the market upon their college and their practice as deep-seated and pernicious. A significant and indicative example of the introduction of business practices into the college is the adoption of industry lead body standards for the key activity of assessing students, carried out by lecturers. Formerly, there were no requirements in place for FE lecturers to hold formal teaching qualifications of any kind, although these were available in a small number of HE and FE institutions providing initial teacher training and in-service certification. Following the introduction of the NCVQ VET framework, it became obligatory for lecturers and others who were involved in assessing students for these awards to have, or to be working towards, the assessor and verifier occupational standards specified by the TDLB. These are commonly known as the 'TDLB awards'. A major part of the case study college staff development budget is allocated for TDLB training and most lecturers are registered by the college with an awarding body for the appropriate qualifications.

The TDLB awards are themselves part of the NCVQ framework and are understood by the lecturers in the study to be specified at Level 3 (A-Level equivalent), which seemed to have been a contributory factor towards the suspicion with which they were generally regarded. Another factor is the competence-based model which the qualifications employ, which again leads them to be considered by these lecturers as a low-level award, patronising with regard to lecturers' status and inappropriate to teaching practice within the FE sector.

A major criticism of the qualifications is that they disaggregate processes related to assessment, and that they divorce assessment from subject knowledge. This procedure is consistent with original guidelines issued for those implementing the GNVQ qualifications, which specified that the grades of 'merit' and 'distinction' were to be awarded for processes rather than knowledge displayed by the student. For one lecturer, the implications of this approach make it an inappropriate model for all but low-level training activities: '...it presupposes no specialist knowledge, other than ability to assess. That might be OK with riveting bits of metal, but in other areas it's not going to be possible.'

Another lecturer also mocked the limited scope of the TDLB awards:

> I'm willing to listen to things, I'm always willing to listen to new ideas because I think those are important, but I think it's, yet again, so sort of crabby. I see almost people with quill pens crabbily writing, 'Oh yes, I'm going to do that, yes I'm going to do that'...it doesn't seem to be grown up, it doesn't seem to be expressive, it doesn't seem to be adult.

This view is consistent with that held by another lecturer, that the imposition of the TDLB framework, in view of its very basic level, its competence-based structure, and its apparent lack of status as a qualification for lecturers, is evidence of the de-skilling of FE lecturers.

It is not the process of reviewing and evaluating assessment procedures which is rejected by these lecturers, but the atomistic methods through which the TDLB awards accredit assessment practice which is problematic: 'Well, having attended an introductory workshop on D32 and D33 the work that I as a lecturer am expected to do in no way differs from the work I'm already doing, it's just formalising it on a piece of paper.' Another agreed that 'you're simply being asked to carry on doing what you're already doing'.

Most lecturers, however, welcomed the opportunity of giving scrutiny to the assessment process; the following two opinions are typical: 'I have no problem with assessing anybody, everything is assessed and should be, but it's the criteria by which you're assessed that is debatable.' 'I think the standardisation of certain kinds of techniques, in terms of assessment anyway, is very useful.'

The focus of the TDLB awards, upon the demonstration of competence by particular students on a particular occasion, both undermine the centrality of the process of learning for these lecturers, and encourage an artificial pigeon-holing of students, which is contrary to their normal practice:

> ...we're supposed to examine a strong student and a weak student, or as they call it a special needs student. Now the special needs student would be basically, is somebody who lacks confidence...it doesn't make sense, you can also have a very good student who goes to work on a particular project and lacks confidence in that area, so that's a loophole of it.

The emphasis upon the learning process was a strongly recurring theme for all of the lecturers in this study. The outcome that is considered of value is not the qualification, but the students' engagement in the learning process, skills achieved and progression opportunities. However, there is some concern expressed as to the implication of a government policy on national training targets expressed as percentages of the population gaining accreditation by a specified date. A policy based upon such specific targets is seen to carry with it the danger of reducing the standard required to pass the qualification, in order to meet the pre-specified targets:

...if the government sets a target of so many people passing NVQs by such and such a date, then the only way to meet it is by knowing the quality threshold and passing them all through it... Performance indicators, payment by results – those sort of things have some obvious flaws. It's obviously possible to just pass people, because you get funded that way, even though really you'd fail them...

The lecturers work in a curriculum area which at the time of the study had not yet fully developed NVQs or GNVQs, and their approach to the NVQ framework is chiefly to adopt a 'wait and see' approach: 'I remain open to, you know, I want to see what the lead bodies and so on come up with and actually look at them.'

Another lecturer thought that the principle of occupation-ally-specific NVQs is a good idea, but had reservations about the way in which they have been introduced:

I can see advantages provided the NVQs would be written more specifically for certain areas, rather than just having say an area of sound engineering which covers the majority of just film work and missing out the musically side of it completely, which is – I won't say totally different – but quite a different scale to the sound field. So I think fundamentally it's a good idea but the way they're implementing it is not very good.

The impact of these curriculum developments upon the lecturers in this study extends beyond the proposed transformation of the courses with which they identify their key functions as course leaders and tutors within a course team framework. It was a requirement for lecturers and others who assessed students for NCVQ qualifications to have, or be working towards, the TDLB assessor and verifier awards. The low regard which the lecturers in this study have for the TDLB awards, and their perceived ineffectiveness when applied within the FE sector for distinguishing good practice, are, it is argued, associated with the inappropriate transfer to an educational context of a model devised for and by management in business and industry, rather than with any reluctance on the part of the lecturers to review their assessment procedures. The TDLB assessor and verifier awards accredit key aspects of lecturers' practice, such as assessment of students' work, operation of accreditation of prior learning, co-ordination of assessment and internal verification. The awards have their origin in business and industrial training, and are challenged by the lecturers in this study as inappropriate and counter-productive to the key task of learning and teaching. As one put it:

> Well, I think it's a load of nonsense to be honest. I don't think it has any credence at all. Everybody knows that the college has got to get us through it so they probably will – we'll do a bit to make sure they can, I suppose. I think the whole strategy is off the wall. You know, that something that we've been doing for some time, now they come, now we have to supposedly go through some qualification based on what we already do, well we already do it, what's the whole point, why not just hand it out then and post it to everybody?

It is the extent to which the awards separate out and isolate procedures which are integral to the broader process of review and analysis of lecturers' own practice which is the target for criticism by some lecturers. Others, whilst welcoming the opportunity to spend time focusing upon assessment which their involvement with the awards provided, nonetheless have reservations about the criteria by which assessment practice is to be assessed. Another view is that managers like the TDLB awards because they provide a measurable indicator of staff development activity. There was some concern amongst the lecturers that in giving high priority to registering staff for the TDLB awards, other more valuable development is being denied to them. These data are consistent with the findings of a recent study of lecturers involved in implementing NVQs (Fisher and Pearson 1995). In their interview study of 16 lecturers, many had reservations about competence-based programme design. Whilst noting that aspects of the approach were endorsed (occupationally-related qualifications, flexible learning and the centrality of work experience), 'deep concern and major disappointments were expressed during implementation' (p.45).

None of the lecturer group considered that work towards the TDLB awards has improved their assessment practice. One reason for this may be the practical difficulty with the use of competence-based approaches for assessing the 'softer' skills which distinguish the expert practitioner – such as the exercise of judgement, intuition, weighing-up ethical issues, behaviour under stress, intellectual ability, and balancing competing demands. Such skills are extremely difficult to reproduce – for example by role-play – outside of the work context; they are extremely difficult to infer from observable behaviour; and there is the additional problem of how, in practice, an assessor might observe performance which may occur spontaneously, infrequently or, worse, only in one-to-one contacts or in small group contexts, between lecturers and students. The extent to which these approaches undermine the collaborative effort of successfully diverse teams (Belbin 1981) within the department is also problematic.

Individual competence is not the same as team or overall competence. In contexts such as FE, where team members are interdependent, the search for individual competences as a measure of lecturer effectiveness is misdirected.

The lecturers in this study who rejected the application of low-level competence-based occupational standards to their practice, did so on the grounds that they are reductionist, demeaning, and fail adequately to reflect the range, level, complexity and sophistication of tasks in which they are engaged. One lecturer called it 'reductio ad absurd...taking it down to the basic level of knowledge, I mean, this person can pick up a pipe and put it down, great, but it tells you nothing about what they can do'. The interview data confirm the view that the use of the TDLB competence framework has further evidenced the de-skilling of lecturers by applying what can be regarded as mechanistic and functional competence criteria to the task of assessing and accrediting students.

Criticism of the use of NCVQ Competency Based Education approaches is not limited to their application to lecturer assessment; there is also opposition to their use in determining and defining the limits of the college curriculum. The nomenclature adopted by NCVQ reveals its strong assessment-driven thrust, de-emphasising students, tutors, teaching and courses, in favour of candidates, assessors, qualifications and the workplace.

The term 'candidate' is strongly suggestive of a singularity and instrumentalism which de-emphasises group contexts, shared learning experiences and understanding through enquiry, risk-taking and experimentation. Hyland (1992d) has argued that this reveals the NCVQ's underlying conception of knowledge as essentially something which can be owned, which is a conception of knowledge that is, he says, 'wholly inadequate, viciously materialistic and utterly subversive of educational contexts in which teachers and students are engaged in rational teaching and learning encounters' (p.10). The focus upon qualifications, which can be taken and awarded independently of participation in collaborative learning experiences, de-emphasises the value of such experiences, whilst at the same time undermining the importance of courses and, more especially, the value of the teaching and learning process, which is the territory of expertise for the lecturer. A view expressed by one lecturer is that CBE has brought with it a shift away from 'letting people develop, express and change opinions and points of view about the place they work in and how it should go on and so on'.

Competence-based assessment

A general criticism of criterion-referenced assessment approaches *per se*, of which competence-based assessment is one example, is a direct consequence of their ancestry which is rooted in philosophical positivism and psychological behaviourism:

> In behaviourism, learning is studied only at its observable level and all other terminology or interpretation in terms of hidden entities or mental processes is denied. Early behaviourism was influenced by a philosophical movement known as positivism which dismissed as meaningless all statements which were not empirically verifiable. Accordingly the cardinal educational principle derived from this set of beliefs was that the only meaningful goals of learning and teaching were those which are objectively measurable as observable outcomes. Other aims are dismissed as little more than pious hopes. (Satterley 1989, p.44)

It can be argued that there are many aspects of learning which are not directly observable. A preoccupation with observable phenomena leads to a narrow, restricted and mechanistic model of learning and teaching which excludes the higher order domains of beliefs, attitudes, and values.

The logic of the NCVQ approach, acknowledged by NCVQ itself, is that the breadth and scope of a course or learning programme is determined by the requirement to demonstrate the competences to which it leads:

> The focus and starting point of this new system is different from the one many of us have been used to. It is the competence, the performance which is required, which establishes the baseline and which is specified. Once this has been established, enabling objectives (many of them possibly knowledge-based) can be identified and appropriate learning experiences leading to the competence can be designed. (Ellis and Gorringe 1989, p.10)

Pring (1992) brings out the difference in emphasis between vocational and academic standards which competence-based approaches foster:

> Unlike academic standards, vocational ones are not mysterious entities slowly internalised, requiring a gradual apprenticeship, possessed 'more or less' and in varying degrees. Rather, one either is or is not competent. One can either do the job that is analysed in terms of a range of performances or (as performance indicators show) one cannot... Courses might or might not be necessary for the achievement of competence – the end is logically disconnected from the means. And therefore courses (where they exist) are assessment led. They are but a means to an end. They, unlike the context of academic standards, do not require, as intrinsically necessary, the apprenticeship, the participation in the very activities through which the standards come to be recognised. (p.14)

He also points out that the quest for 'absolute standards' within the core subjects for the General Certificate of Secondary Education (GCSE), the development of attainment targets at ten different levels in the National Curriculum, and the attempts to equate levels of achievement at GCSE and 'A' level with levels of NVQs, are all manifestations of the same desire to equate standards with competence criteria or 'fitness for purpose'. Quite simply, the competency model is inadequate to the task of assessing any but the most basic skill or task whose complete performance can be described in terms of observable, empirically verifiable outcomes. That is, the standard to be specified is absolute. However, it is arguable that even some basic skills cannot be so reduced and assessed in terms of an 'absolute' standard. Within the NCVQ framework, for example:

> ...either you can or you cannot turn a piece of wood at level 2. You either are or are not competent. There is no room for shades of competence – or at least, where there are such shades they are thought to be a defect in the analysis, not a reflection of things as they are. And yet quality is often reflected in such adverbial qualifications of competence (or 'can do's') as 'elegantly', 'gracefully', 'imaginatively', intelligently', creatively'. Such adverbs imply judgement which is irreducible to the application of pre-conceived performance indicators. (Pring 1992, pp.15–16)

A further difficulty is that the assessment of competence is no straightforward matter:

> Assessment of competence *by anyone* is fraught with difficulties. Competence is hard to define and is open to interpretation. What, for example, degree of infallibility is required before we accept that someone is really competent? Does the ability to type a letter with acceptable accuracy today mean that the operator concerned will be capable of doing so again tomorrow or next year? (Needham 1988, p.46)

NCVQ, in describing competence in terms of performance, subsumes competence within performance. The NCVQ model blurs a crucial distinction between competence and performance. The *locus classicus* of the competence/performance dichotomy is in Chomskian linguistics (Chomsky 1971). Linguistic competence is that part of a speaker's knowledge of the language system ('langue' in Saussure's terms) which enables the production of language. Performance, on the other hand, refers to actual language behaviour and this is influenced by contextual factors such as social conventions, emotion, social and situational context, and beliefs. The distinction which Chomsky draws between competence and performance is similar to Saussure's distinction between 'langue' and 'parole'. Both Chomsky's and Saussure's distinctions have been heavily criticised, which itself serves to underline the complexity of the relationship between competence and performance. Certainly any conflation of the two is theoretically unsound.

The rationale for competence-based approaches to assessing performance in the workplace is that there are generic competences underlying all jobs. Boyatzis (1982) one of the pioneers of the management competence movement in the USA, justified the development of a competence-based model of effective management by defining competence as an underlying characteristic which may be apparent in a wide variety of different observable actions and forms of behaviour. The emphasis here is upon the capability which is causally related to effective and/or superior performance: 'A person's set of competencies reflect his or her capability. They are describing what he or she *can do*, not necessarily what he or she does, nor does all the time regardless of the situation and setting' (p.23).

NCVQ (1988), building on the Training Agency approach, adopted a definition of competence which focused more centrally upon observable actions and behaviours: 'The ability to perform work activities to the standards required in employment.'

A lead body for FE

Garland (1994) has suggested that the problems of applying lead body standards to the teaching role in further and higher education (FHE) can be ameliorated through the involvement of practitioners in setting the standards, and more painstaking attention to the real complexities and dilemmas of teaching. However, we are left with the criticism of Competency Based Education, which Moss (1981) first exposed, that the observable parts of tasks describe neither their complete nor even their most significant elements in most cases. The key point is that the TA/NCVQ definitions of competence, by embracing skills and abilities, are limited by their own terms of reference to actions and behaviours which can be observed and empirically verified. Hyland (1992d), in examining the implications of such a competency model for adult education, legitimately questions its epistemological basis: 'Clearly, there is something unsatisfactory about a theoretical perspective which apparently recognises knowledge and understanding only to the extent that these are revealed in the performance of occupational tasks' (p.9).

The competency movement, then, has profound implications for the nature of education and training; the consequences for educational institutions are similarly profound. One nightmare vision is that of a 'cafeteria' model of educational institutions, where customers pick and mix from budget-priced units and quantify their experience and prior learning in training credits. In the area of management, this process has been described as: '...a disaggregation process that reduces management to an amorphous bundle of elements each with their own performance criteria. This is like using a quantity surveyor rather than an artist to capture the grandeur of St Paul's Cathedral' (Everard and Morris 1990, p.15).

This graphically makes the fundamental point which underlines many specific criticisms of CBE: that pre-specified performance criteria are not appropriate as the reference point for the assessment of managerial, professional and other 'higher order' work roles. It is, therefore, a matter of some concern that, at the time of writing, consultation is underway on government proposals (strongly supported by college employers) for a lead body for further education which would develop occupational standards for teaching and other work roles. The Further Education Development Agency has been commissioned to carry out a functional and occupational mapping exercise of FE occupations (teaching and support staff) with a view to specifying possible standards to be developed. The functional map produced by such an exercise is unlikely to view teaching as a co-intentional, transactional process in which both student and teacher engage as equal participants (Freire 1972).

It appears likely that government has in mind the eventual establishment of an education lead body that would specify common competence-based occupational standards for all educational practitioners and that the FE sector has been chosen as a soft target for a pilot exercise, since a number of occupational roles carried out within the sector – such as Customer Service, Training and Development – already fall within the NVQ framework. It is unrealistic to expect that the performance criteria which are determined by the FE lead body will be less narrow and prescriptive than those produced so far for other occupations, or that they will extend beyond a technicistic summary of the most instrumental and directly observable competences associated with the lecturer role. The danger of this is that once teaching is defined in such terms, the status and esteem of the lecturer as a reflective practitioner is in question. College managers may well be tempted to replace highly trained and experienced lecturing staff for part-time agency lecturers or technician-demonstrators who can carry out effective performance of a limited range of so-called 'lecturer competencies', who do not belong to teaching unions which are organised in colleges, who can be easily hired and fired, and whose contribution will include reducing the organisation's expenditure on human resources (Elliott and Hall 1994).

An alternative model of teaching in FE

An alternative model of teaching which avoids the pitfalls noted above is more fully articulated in Chapter 6. However, the point is made here that one way forward would be to forego reductionist notions of teaching which disaggregate the lecturer role, thereby reducing it to a simplistic collection of discrete competences, in favour of a strategy which recognises the diversity and complexity of the role and the sensitivity and reflectiveness required of those who effectively carry it out. A good place to start would be to look at the language of the tributes paid to effective teaching by pupils and students and to note the frequency with which such perceptions are described in whole person attributes. The centrality of biography, personality and identity to the teaching role has only recently been fully recognised (see, for example, Huberman 1993; Goodson 1994; Hargreaves 1994). The model of teaching which underpins such work is one which fully recognises the importance of the notion of empowerment of teaching staff. Fundamental to this is a view of staff which is diametrically opposed to the hard Human Resource Management theories which inform the description and analysis of teaching as an occupation characterised simply by the performance of competences.

The view presented by Garland (1994), that competence-based approaches to teacher education 'enable a basis from which to develop learner-centred approaches and to allow greater learner autonomy' (pp.17–18) is disingenuous. Competence Based Education in the United Kingdom has not so far

realised these advantages, but as Garland himself acknowledges, has brought about 'over-prescription in the assessment
specification and unnecessary bureaucracy' (p.19). The consistent focus upon learning outcomes, rather than learning processes, has led to the situation where professional development
is undervalued, and uncoupled from accreditation. Regardless
of how much teacher educators may encourage participation in
group-based, open-ended learning experiences, it is improbable
that lecturers as 'resourceful humans' (Bottery 1992), rather than
'people', in the incorporated FE sector, will either be empowered
or funded by their managers to participate in such professional
development.

The development of NVQs in teaching, tutoring, learning
support and so on would bring about a radical overhaul of the
initial teacher training (ITT) and in-service training (INSET)
curriculum, bringing both ITT and INSET within the NCVQ
framework. The de-skilling of teachers and lecturers, and the
dominance of a rationalist curriculum, will have been confirmed
and consolidated. The implications of such developments for
policy and practice in schools, colleges and universities suggest
an agenda for educational policy studies and research, and
highlight the importance, for all educational practitioners, of
addressing, as a matter of urgency, the implications of competence-based approaches to the definition and assessment of
working practice.

CHAPTER SIX

Lecturers and Managers

The purpose of this chapter is to highlight the deep-seated concerns of the lecturers in the case study college about current management practices. The evidence for these concerns within the interview transcripts is presented, but the chapter also presents the possibilities of an alternative model of management, more consistent with a pedagogic frame of reference.

FE lecturers and student learning

A major theme, which was returned to frequently by all lecturers in the study, is that of the need to keep students at the centre of the educational process. Whilst recognising the need for efficient and effective management in colleges, they were increasingly fearful of a shift in the core business and focus of colleges, from the development of students' potential to a preoccupation with balancing the budget. The majority of the lecturers in the study, on the other hand, expressed the view that 'the students should be priority'. This led them to share a concern that the vocationalisation of the FE curriculum is endangering the educational character of FE provision, shifting the focus of provision away from serving the needs of the students to serving the needs of the labour market. As one lecturer put it:

> ...I have a concern about the move to totally competence-based and vocationally-based focus within the FE sector. I regret there is some loss in losing that kind of general educational background that always did exist...I mean I do recognise the need for a skills-based workforce in the country, but my perception of the successful economies is that

they not only skills-based but they also have a level of understanding and awareness across a range of issues...

Another condemned the drift within vocational education towards basic, vocational skills, and away from a more rounded, higher level, education:

> ...some of that critical edge is being lost and a lot of courses are much more to be concerned, I suppose, with how to use those manipulative skills rather (than)...to understand why that process of persuasion is taking place and to understand something about the ideological notions that are ascribed to certain forms of communication, etc.

Most lecturers understood that they have a responsibility to look beyond the immediate needs of industry, as identified in labour market surveys and the like, to future economic patterns and, crucially, to the needs of the *students* in relation to those future trends. The following extract underlines the extent to which the lecturers are concerned to ensure that their everyday practices articulate with the needs of the wider market within which colleges operate:

> ...looking at education as a whole and seeing where education should be going, looking at the students in the group and thinking, 'what do they need, what's out in the current market, what's going to be happening five or ten years down the road?' Trying to predict rather than accepting what's happening now, and just trying to get through day-to-day.

The emphasis, for this lecturer, should be upon review, renewal, innovation and discovery, as opposed to time-serving and focusing upon paper qualifications:

> ...if all the students come out with, oh nothing, they just come out with a qualification, but no inspiration, no motivation, what's the point of that with the art form? And I think that should be the same for any area, whether it's maths or physics or you know – there's still got to be something new to be discovered and when you've got somebody sitting on a pedestal, who ends up telling you: 'you shouldn't do that, that's too dangerous. Why don't you just play safe and do A, B, C, D?' Fine, but it's not developing.

All lecturers in the study perceived that they have a facilitative, enabling role in working with students, and typically expressed this role in terms of a student-centred pedagogy: '...enabling students can be a simple process of orientation through delivery and then they start to use themselves and any kind of physical and library resources and yourself as a resource, and they're up and running'.

The high value placed by the lecturers upon creativity leads them to a highly democratic notion of the lecturer/student relationship:

> I find the easiest way for a student to understand is for them to create themselves, whether it's a product – you know a large-scale production or whether it's a scale model of something – or whether it's their own ideas. I mean I always say to students: 'none of your ideas are wrong.'

Thus were students encouraged to develop a critical, questioning intelligence which enables them to 'understand what processes they're being subjected to'.

The emphasis within this model of teaching, highlighted by most lecturers, is not upon the omnipotent and all-knowing lecturer, nor upon the content of what is taught. It is, rather, upon the process in which lecturers and students equally engage. In this engagement, the relationship is not expressed as one which involves lecturers filling students with subject knowledge. One lecturer described his role as one of a facilitator in an educational setting providing access to knowledge – which is not the same as providing knowledge[1] – and also ensuring essential feedback into the process. Another put it in terms of his responsibility for creating an appropriate learning environment, which provides progression opportunities.

The model which emerges from the interview data is a long way from the idea of the lecturer as someone who pours knowledge into empty students: '...we're not here to lecture – er, and we're not here to teach – we're here to access knowledge. So I see lecturers as facilitators, people who can provide opportunities to access knowledge'.

This widely shared student-centred pedagogic framework denies a narrow, prescriptive and mechanistic view of the task

---

1   As Dr Johnson noted, 'Knowledge is of two kinds. We know a subject ourselves, or we know where we can find information upon it' (*Boswell's Life of Johnson* Ed. G B Hill, revised edn. L F Powell, 1934, p.365).

of further education, and insists that it 'should be about enabling individuals to...not fit that system, not to socialise them, but to train them in ways that they can be critical about that system, because only by being critical can you make progress'.

Lecturers are required to apply the same standards to their own practice as they do to students: 'I don't see lecturers as omnipotent and knowing everything. I think a good lecturer always admits when they don't know something. If they don't know they'll go away and find out, because you expect a student to do that so why shouldn't you do that.'

Managerialism

A practical consequence of the broadly-conceived student-fo-cused model of teaching supported by these lecturers is that classroom contact is seen to be central to the education process. Attempts by college managers to meet deadlines imposed upon them by the FEFC and others, by cascading paperwork – including Management Information System data returns, multiple registers – and other requests for information, are largely re-sisted by these lecturers on the grounds that they are time-con-suming, of little immediate or longer-term relevance to their practice, and wasteful of time that could be more usefully spent with students or on curriculum-based tasks.

One reaction to the increasing demands for paperwork is to withdraw co-operation, which is seen to be a reasonable strategy falling short of active resistance. Most lecturers are dilatory in their observation of paper systems, and ascribe the reason for this to the failure of college managers to understand and appre-ciate their problems and the nature of their day-to-day work: 'The type of work that I think we're trying to undertake here, and the type of considerations that we are preparing to under-take here, doesn't seem wholly compatible with the kind of management-led, rather hard-nosed culture that seems to ema-nate from [main site].'

Another lecturer perceived that managers have 'a lack of understanding of the courses the college are actually running'. This is a commonly held view. This lecturer's first impressions of the college are proved to be mistaken, as his experience of working as a full-time lecturer gradually revealed a mismatch between the aims of college managers and those of lecturing staff:

> I was under the impression that the college was fully behind the lecturing staff, and that if a lecturer's keen to do his job to the fullest extent they would get a lot of support and encouragement to actually go ahead and to actually strive for the students, but that doesn't appear to be always the case.

The lack of support felt by lecturing staff gave rise to a frustration based upon a perception that college management has little purchase upon the core activity of teaching and the associated resource requirements which are seen as vital to the successful implementation of lecturers' practice:

> We scratch around for things for the students, they spend things on themselves and that is a big mistake – it may be indicative of their attitude to their role, and it could be that in their greatly exalted position they see student needs as less important than lecturers do. I think that is probably a moral issue...

The teaching of students was seen to be undervalued by college managers and a distance is put between them and lecturers and students through the creation of unnecessary hierarchical college structures. The problem with such structures for lecturers is that they are self-serving, and management practice becomes an end in itself, at a distance from lecturers, teaching and learning, whilst students are marginalised:

> ...it actually sets up, again, the idea that management is more important than the lecturing or the teaching, that management is an end in itself – which it isn't – management is there to serve the institution which is there to serve the students. It seems to me it's distancing from the ideal of the students... Students are referred to not as students, FE something...FTEs,[2] yeah. I hate that. It makes me mad, it's not an FTE, it's a student, it's not a numerical unit, it's a student. That to me is both symptomatic and symbolic of a managerial attitude which should have nothing to do with education.

---

2   Full Time Equivalents

Symbolic practices, so described, reveal a context of misunder-standing and miscommunication. In expanding upon the gulf which he perceived to exist between lecturers and college managers, this lecturer makes clear that it is not simply a matter of poor communication; he believes there are deep-seated ideological differences:

> A managerial style has to show that it's operating on the same wave-length as you are, it's not enough to assume it, yes, there should be people taking care of the business, but you need to have the confidence and the faith that they're taking care of the business in the way that you believe in, that is in accord with your philosophy, with a philosophy of education, which I'm not confident that it is...

This difference in philosophical orientation between college managers and lecturers recurs as a theme in the accounts of most lecturers in the study. One lecturer commented upon the management style of senior managers as 'heavy handed' and 'hierarchical', whereas he felt that the management role should try 'to enable lecturers to do the work they want to do with the least difficulty, given the interference from government'.

These differences of perception as to the purpose and function of college managers find their expression in the identification of a range of issues of contention, including tight control of resources, poor communication, lack of staff consultation, reactive and autocratic agenda-setting, and brinkmanship. These issues underline the twin concerns of lecturers, first that incorporation has brought about an FE structure which pushes managers to adopt what were seen as hard business-oriented strategies, particularly in relation to HRM, and second, that management decisions are taken at too great a distance from the level of practice of the lecturers. Both concerns were expressed by this lecturer:

> ...there seems to me to be, the overriding concern of management at the moment is not to spend any money. They put in place what they have to put in place, strategic plans and the like, supposedly by consultation, but even that's different to what's put in and the management seems to have taken it upon themselves to change things, presumably because they consider themselves to be in a better position and to know what our target ought to be in terms of student

numbers... The staff seem to think of them, or the ones I've spoken to, almost like running about like headless chickens, running around panicking about the latest issue, and shouting to somebody about it, and responding to crises rather than having a definite, an active plan to invigorate the institute and get it operating the way it will meet whatever plans they lay out...they stay up there, they don't respond to memos, they don't meet meetings unless they want to, and they seem to have to be pushed right to the edge to actually do anything.

The suspicion and hostility towards senior management, which is recorded within most lecturers' accounts, is variously attributed to managers' poor communication, lack of direction, anxiety and incompetence. One lecturer detected a management strategy which seems to be 'based on a kind of brinkmanship and crisis'. Another called the management style 'confrontational'.

Lecturers in this study are not seeking to carp against and criticise management for its own sake. The difficulties and pressures under which colleges have to operate, following incorporation and the subsequent loss of external support systems previously provided by the LEAs, are recognised:

I think senior management need to remind themselves from time to time that a lot of what is being imposed, is being imposed on them as well, is being imposed by government directive...people that go on to senior management, and are responsible for cross-college applications of their skills and so on – I think that's a bloody difficult job – at the same time I do think it's their job to find out as much as possible about those areas, I think some do, but I don't think it's common enough.

What is not considered acceptable are circumstances where college managers fail to take account of the specialist and particular needs of curriculum areas, which represent the primary context in which the lecturer is enabled to interact – or prevented from interacting – with the students. As one lecturer put it:

I certainly have a concern that there isn't an understanding, or that there is no particular attempt by senior management to understand the particular strategies that are needed to deliver the area that I'm interested in and am responsible for teaching and that, if you like, what there seems to be all the time is an attempt to fit everybody into a sort of common box, so that teaching is something that you do in a certain kind of way, it doesn't matter what the content is or what the subject matter is, or even what vocational area it's related to, you do it in the same kind of way...

A bottom-up model of management

The primary focus of this study is upon the lecturers' worldview. The hostility expressed by many lecturers towards the top-down style of management practised in this college is strongly evidenced within the interview data. Yet there is an equally strong theme emerging from the data which points to a viable, alternative model of management derived from the lecturers' perspective and grounded in pedagogical culture. At the same time, it is a model which is realistic in that it recognises a competitive environment and the consequent need for the college to be well-run. Whilst most lecturers voiced strong opposition to the idea of the college as a business, they well appreciate the extent to which it is necessary for the organisation to be efficient, and to be run in a businesslike manner, in order to be effective: 'I believe in efficiently run organisations, but I don't believe in "efficiency" and "in business" being a priority which overrides the concerns and the needs of students and, in fact, of staff as well... There is a place for this, business management is important.'

The position represented by this lecturer, and others, is not that management is unnecessary, but that 'progress has to be linked to what is best for the student, not to what's best for the business, (so) that managerial team needs to bear in mind all the time what that business is for and who the business is for'.

The key point is the differential emphasis placed by lecturers and managers upon business and educational values. Lecturers feel that, for the college managers, business methods have become an end in themselves, sustaining a 'control' ethos and a managerialist culture. A common complaint is that college managers seem to have lost sight of the core business of student learning and achievement – they no longer see students as students, but as units of funding. On the other hand the lecturers in this group prioritise learning and teaching processes. Crucially, however, they are not unaware of the need for the college to be competitive in the newly created quasi-market, or naïve about the need for management efficiency. One lecturer showed a sharp sense of realism in relation to the funding of his curriculum area: 'I know that funding is going to be tight and therefore you try and do the best you can within that circumstance to try and do the things you want to do within a particular department, and if you can't do it one way you find another way to achieve it.'

Another considered that whilst the college management do not know where to contract, 'it knows where to expand but is very cautious about putting the money forward (quite rightly – that's good business practice)'.

A third acknowledged that colleges should be externally accountable, but with the enigmatic caveat that accountability must be consistent with high standards:

> Part of me says yes, I mean any industrial body who are investing money into colleges should expect a certain standard when they have people trained by the college. My other half says that's fine but if the college has got to cut corners to try and meet those standards or if the college standards were above that which the industry were expecting I don't think they should cut them. I believe they should try and acquire the highest standard possible for the students.

Whilst incorporation has heightened, and to a large extent symbolised, the encroachment of a market in further education, it is important to note that its effects are not uniformly regarded negatively by this group of lecturers. There is a view, which the following extracts illustrate, that independence can bring certain advantages:

> I suppose that as far as experience goes in practice it is rather early days...freedom from various changes in political control could be an advantage.

> I think there are advantages in institutions having the freedom to decide what they should do without artificial constraints and without the mix-and-match funding that you've had before. In theory I think it was an excellent idea and I was strongly in favour of it...

Even for some of the lecturers with major reservations concerning incorporation, some of the effects are regarded as potentially short-lived. A poor response to staffing requests led one lecturer to express a 'hope that that was simply a matter of incorporation and it just happened and they were sorting out themselves, and that now that would have happened a lot better this time'.

A benefit of incorporation was thought by one lecturer to be the extent to which it can foster ownership of strategic planning by management: 'Now if under incorporation they're free to a certain extent to decide what changes to take place you can expect a sense of ownership from the management, which might result in them presenting it more positively.'

One lecturer identified the lack of training and development received by college managers to prepare them for change, rather than incorporation itself, as the underlying issue: 'I think senior management of all institutions have been well dropped in it by the Government...because they've had no training, because they've had no development.'

Insofar as the lecturers are critical of management, there are also signs that most lecturers have a shared and clear view of what would constitute an appropriate model of college management. It would be sensitive to the primary concerns of lecturers:

> From my point of view, if a management team is responsible for running a college there should be certain people responsible within that upper management circle for being acquainted with the needs of every course, so they should be able to monitor those needs, to see if they are adequately funded or to see if they're being over funded, i.e. draw back some of the money from them, and, if you like, they should be accountable for the way in which college funds are spent and for the efficiency of sites and the general efficiency of the college. Making sure the advertising is quite right to attract the students to fill the courses that are on offer, and, if you like, investigate possible growth areas for them.

It follows from this that there should be common ownership of the strategic plan: '(Linking institutional and personal development) seems to me very sensible with certain caveats because that presupposes that everybody in the institution shares ownership of the strategic plan and if that doesn't happen then there are going to be problems with the strategic plan.'

There is a widely shared view that managers should communicate their own values to lecturers: 'You know it's perfectly likely that there are people here who are very sympathetic to the needs and aims of the college senior management...if anybody ever told us what they were.'

This gives further weight to the argument that the lecturers are not operating in an isolated or idealistic context; they understand the demands made by incorporation upon management, but find their own value-orientation undermined by the way in which senior managers embrace the use of a new educational management jargon, which reflects the needs of accountancy rather than pedagogy and exacerbates the problem of communication of management purposes:

> It may be a problem in educational management that our changes are never presented that well...I have to say that part of their problem is that they don't communicate very well with the staff... I mean I don't think they communicate what their plans are, they don't actually have a presence in the college.

Many of the management failings that are mentioned by the lecturer group are seen to emanate from an inconsistent and unclear approach to the management of the college. The following extracts again show an awareness of the need for management, but take issue with the lack of clarity and purposefulness displayed by senior management: 'I'd much prefer a strategy that was clear and I disagreed with than the apparent confusion and fog that we are suffering from at the moment.' Another lecturer agreed that clarity of management style is important:

> I feel if I knew what it was, if it was simple, top-down line management or whatever, based on whatever comes down from the top I could at least cope with it, but just as you feel that you've got a grip on whatever particular style is being employed this week it seems to be different the next week.

The issues of clear decision-making, individual managerial responsibility and effective communication are clearly highlighted within the following extract as both significant and problematic within the context of the case study college:

> ...you need to know who...has a brief for a particular problem that happens to be on your desk at that particular moment. You may not need to take it to senior management,

but you need to know that if you did – or if it got to that stage, or if you couldn't deal with it or whatever that happened – it takes you days to find out and, when you have found out or you think you've found out, then it's not actually them. And what does concern me that it seems that most of the...senior managers of the college, are behaving as though they are simply advisors, in other words if you've got a problem then they can advise you on various routes you might take, but they won't make a decision. Now that seems to me fine at (departmental) level, but it's not fine at senior management level because I don't go to a senior manager unless I've got something that I really need to say: 'look this, quite clearly, is your responsibility and I need you to make a decision, can you ring me back and let me know?' You don't go to senior managers for any other reason, I've no need to, there's really not a great deal of point. And there's not a great deal of encouragement here to have an ongoing sort of dialogue with senior management.

It is clear from what this lecturer said that the model of management which is being rejected is one which does not assume responsibility for the effective communication and implementation of its policies. A 'dialogue' is expected, even assumed, and it is largely the absence of opportunities to engage in dialogue which drives wedges between lecturers and senior managers. The formalised management style adopted by senior managers, the embracing of business jargon, the use of confrontation politics in the run-up to incorporation, and the sense which the lecturers have that management do not understand, care about, or value the curriculum activity, all contribute in a major way to stifling dialogue and prevent even beginning to build upon the areas of commonality which exist.

The evidence of emergent and oppositional cultures within the data reported in this chapter direct analysis towards the existence of a shared lecturer culture and its characteristics. This territory seems a fruitful one to pursue, since lecturers themselves clearly feel that the cultural dimension is important to the successful implementation of their role within the incorporated college. It also appears significant since the extent and degree of change which college managers are asking lecturers to take on, including acceptance of new contracts with more flexible working arrangements and the operation of a new qualifications framework, appear to be in jeopardy for as long as cultural-political differences between lecturers and college managers are allowed to persist unaddressed.

A pedagogic culture

It is difficult to overestimate the genuine concern and frustration felt by lecturing staff at the position in which college managers have been placed by government policy for the FE sector, and at the ways in which their managers have chosen to interpret and carry through their tasks. Whether the senior management were predisposed to a managerialist ethos prior to incorporation is beyond the scope of this study to determine. What seems clear, however, is that incorporation has provided both an impetus and a rationale for such an ethos. The lecturers are left with an overwhelming feeling of frustration, which is summed up by the comment: '…the staff aren't motivated because they don't know what the heck's happening because of incorporation, because it's a business now.'

Lecturers feel at odds with the increasing dominant managerialist culture, evidenced by HRM approaches to college management; the use of quality assurance systems, which prioritised business methodology which lecturers find alien and inappropriate; the application of the TDLB awards to a critical aspect of the teaching role itself and the perceived reductionist character of these awards; and the undermining of the very task of teaching and engaging in shared learning experiences with students, through the adoption of a competence-based qualification framework under NCVQ which prioritises work-based experience over classroom experience.

Lecturers themselves, on the other hand, within this study, manage to maintain a view of their task which enables them to satisfy the increasing calls upon them to meet the requirements of industry, whilst at the same time preserving a strong student-centred focus. The interview data point to a model of teaching and learning which is collaborative, affirms equality of status between lecturer and student, and which privileges the exercise of a critical intelligence as an essential part of the preparation of students for higher education and employment. This model is, it can be seen, one which is very appropriate for the FE sector, where an increasing proportion of students are mature adults who are returning to an education system which may have failed them in the past. It is one which can meet the objectives and preferred learning outcomes specified by NCVQ, but in ways which give added value, over and above a narrow mechanistic following of an outcome-based competency framework.

A significant achievement of these lecturers is to achieve success in examination results for their students, whilst at the same time rejecting the narrow definition of their role which seems to them to be introduced through the imposition of business culture within the college. The strong sense of dismay and outrage felt by the lecturers, in this study, at the lack of understanding and communication on the part of the college management provides a sharp counterpoint to their view of the appropriate relationships to be developed with students.

It is perhaps not surprising, at a time when educational values and the value of education seem to be under maximum threat from policy-driven initiatives – directed towards the achievement of national training targets – and externally imposed performance indicators, that lecturers have been concerned to articulate and confirm their commitment to a counter-balancing theoretical orientation which underpinned their practice and sustained it in the face of a strong managerialist alternative. This orientation was expressed in terms of a student-centred approach shared by the lecturers in the department which is the focus of this study.

However, it is significant that the lecturers in this study are prepared to go along with the notion of the application of performance indicators and formal quality assurance procedures to their work in the creative arts. In the case of the TDLB awards, they are criticised less for their intention than for the language associated with them and their wholesale introduction in what is seen to be an inappropriate and insensitive manner. Very similar objections are raised about the introduction of quality assurance systems in general, and BS5750 in particular. The lecturers are not against the notion of external accountability, or the need to formally assure the quality of the curriculum offer. One lecturer, who had previously worked in arts organisations, could see no problem in applying performance indicators to education:

Again I really don't have a problem with applying some sort
of judgement as to whether things are successful or unsuc-
cessful – we do it all the time in the theatre and we know
very well in theatre, more so than you do in fine art – that if
you have something that people don't like they won't come
and you have an empty house the second night and we test
our ideas whether we have achieved what we set out to do...
How you do that we can discuss, but I don't mind my
performance being judged.

Another lecturer, who was consistently critical of the importa-
tion of business procedures like BS5750 into education, nonetheless understood, through his experience of working in fringe
theatre, the demands of the market upon non-profit organisations: '...organisations like small theatre companies have been
forced to become much more businesses.'

None of the lecturers had concerns over the use of external
assessment and evaluation of aspects of their work. The following comment is typical: '...if a performance indicator is assessed
externally it seems to me that whether or not you agree with the
criteria which is being assessed, it is at least a genuine assessment.'

Similarly, there was general agreement amongst these lecturers that management appraisal of lecturers could be a positive
process as long as it is carried out at an appropriate level and by
appropriate people:

...it seems to me that appraisal is a perfectly reasonable
process to take place as it does in industry and so on and
elsewhere... I have no objection in principle to an appraisal
system, but I think it has to be seen as very positive not as a
very basic level of checking people's competencies and ability.

I think appraisals are a good idea, but there's always a
danger that if it has to be by other professionals who are
involved within the field, rather than someone who has no
knowledge of the technicalities of the course that's going
on... I mean I wouldn't like it to happen very often, but I
would think that every so often it's fair.

The lecturers were highly supportive of applying the process of
monitoring and review to all their activities, and recognised the

need to formalise the process in order to ensure that time is allocated to it:

> I think monitoring of what you're doing is fine. I've got no objection to appraisal at all, in fact I welcome it quite often, appraisal is an opportunity for you to appraise what you're doing, you don't always have time unless there is a system that enables you to make time to do that, so I'm actually in favour of it.

Similarly, there is evidence to suggest that these lecturers would support an approach, such as that used within the 'Investors in People' initiative, where individual needs are evaluated in light of their correspondence with the needs of the organisation: '...your training or your personal development will be supported as long as it fits in with the organisation. That's the same with any organisation...you only get things paid for that benefit the organisation.'

In their relationship with their students, the lecturers reject the trappings of the market and the language of business and perceive of themselves as co-investigators; their language reflects notions of sharing, participating, and exploring with students. As one put it, 'you're throwing lots of responsibility back onto the students and you're fighting with that responsibility, you're giving them the choice...'. On the other hand, in their relationship with college managers, the lecturers seem to feel themselves to be the oppressed – of little value, recipients of top-down communication, and not to be trusted or taken into confidence.

Faced with this situation, it is the reflective practice of the lecturers which enables them to sustain a sense of value and worthwhileness in terms of their interaction with students, and in the strategies which they employ in order to ensure that the relationship with students and the teaching and learning process are not diminished. The lecturers are thus engaged in a political struggle on behalf of their students, who are being let down and failed by a system in process of being re-designed by college managers to serve the needs of administration and managerialism rather than of pedagogy and learning.

The collaborative teaching and learning model suggested by the data is very close to Freire's (1972) notion of co-intentional education introduced in Chapter Two. Co-intentional education involves teacher and student sharing knowledge and developing together with equal status as subjects. The banking model of education, on the other hand, conceives of knowledge as a product or commodity which can be measured and given a credit or tariff value. It is a model central to the present funding methodology adopted in FE and underpinned by the use of quantitative performance indicators and quality assurance systems.

Co-intentional and banking models of educational practice both describe and explain the relationships between teaching staff and students on the one hand and college managers on the other. By according the teaching and learning process the highest priority, the lecturers in this study are asserting the relevance and importance of their expertise and, at the same time, rejecting the imposed business ethic which would dilute their contribution.

Notwithstanding the lecturers' suspicion of the managerialist education, they are, in practice, realistically aware of the competitive environment in which they work but, nonetheless, are at pains to prioritise what they see as the core business. The view of education as a 'product' which they give or pass on to students is rejected by these lecturers. By asserting the centrality of a pedagogical orientation which centres upon students' needs, lecturers present a powerful alliance for managing change. Educational policy and managerialist strategies which are regarded by them as subversive of critical pedagogy are resisted. On the other hand, opportunities to underline their pedagogical orientation, through adaptation or other strategies, are seldom missed, in order to buttress their position within the institution and safeguard the arena of their expertise.

Central to all this is the political dimension of the lecturers' critical pedagogy. The aim of it is to direct themselves and their students towards an understanding of the socio-economic conditions within which teaching and learning take place. In other words, to develop an understanding that education is political in nature. Attempts to undervalue the contribution and role of lecturers, to limit the curriculum to a narrow range of vocationally related competences, and to gauge the effectiveness of the FE college by a set of quantitative indicators derived from manufacturing industry, are manifestations of the politicisation

of education which has been launched by the present Conservative administration and perpetrated by college managers who
have been given little option but to implement governmental
reforms, often with little training or development to support
them in the task.

It was noted in Chapter Two that Freire's notion of 'conscientisation' refers to the development of a critical consciousness to
a level where individuals can achieve a sufficient degree of social
and political awareness to understand contradictions within
society and to work to transform it. This notion is in accord with
the rationale used by the lecturers in this study for the priority
which they accord in a working day to engagement with their
students. Many of the lecturers frequently speak in terms of
'empowering' students and making them aware of the economic
and social influences upon them. One lecturer saw his role as to
encourage in students 'an understanding of being able to read
and interpret the things that they see and do…because it shapes
their perceptions'. No lecturers, however, perceived of this role
in isolation. The changing context of the FE sector, and the
internal changes within the college, gives the framework for the
lecturers' actions and underlines, in many cases, the critical
importance of holding onto a learner-centred perspective. These
twin concerns were put into focus by this lecturer:

> …there are institutional needs, but a good lecturer should
> take institutional needs into account. That to me is part of
> the definition of somebody who's worth the job or not. They
> have to constantly balance those institutional needs with
> student needs and whatever individual needs of course,
> that's part of the process.

It is the high level of awareness in relation to the social and
institutional context of action which lends weight to the notion
of conscientisation which is characterised by critical enquiry,
rather than pre-formed answers.

The importance which Freire accords to communication and
dialogue, in allowing individuals to realise their humanity, resonates strongly both with the lecturers' belief in developing
rapport and dialogue with students and with their resentment
at the refusal or inability of senior management to communicate
its strategies and policies to the staff as a whole. As one lecturer
noted, 'there seems to be no respect for the teaching staff at all…

They are not prepared to take an interest in what courses involve, I mean to personally come down and see what's happening'.

For Freire, the development of a critical awareness of self is a central task which is achieved by the development of 'praxis' – the synthesis between reflection and action. This squares the circle, for it is here that we return to the notion of the lecturer as a reflective practitioner and repeat the key point that reflective practice is a political act.

It should be pointed out that Freire's notions of critical pedagogy, praxis and conscientisation are lenses through which the lecturers' reported views are interpreted, rather than terms which they themselves use. The value of the notions, however, is in identifying a basis for an FE-located educational theory which is grounded in the central concern of lecturers, namely teaching and learning as reflective practice – as a political and self-critical process – and locating this in relation to existing theoretical analysis.

This chapter has presented an analysis and interpretation of the data which has been suggestive of the existence of a pedagogic culture amongst a group of FE lecturers. This culture has been characterised as embodying a perspective of reflective practice which balances a concern with the improvement of the quality of the student learning experience with an understanding of – and a pragmatic, measured response to – the reality of a competitive market in education. It has been argued that this perspective influences lecturers' responses to prevalent policy trends in a college which is run by senior managers with a strong managerialist culture. It has been suggested that managerialist and pedagogic cultures co-exist in this college, creating and sustaining tensions which are fuelled by failures in communication. The cultural-political aspect of reflective practice has again been highlighted, and it is this theme, and the potential of qualitative research for exploring it, to which the final chapter addresses itself.

CHAPTER SEVEN

Conclusions

Understanding Teaching in FE and its Importance as a Management Issue

This final chapter draws together and focuses the key themes and issues raised by the study, and highlights their strategic importance for college lecturers and managers. The first two sections highlight the implications of the study for lecturers and managers in the FE sector, whilst a third section explores the potential of qualitative research methods for management studies and the staff development of college managers. It is suggested that qualitative research and evaluation methodologies can both be illuminative for college managers in revealing the epistemology underlying the current preference for a rational-technical managerialism and valuable for them in establishing alternative criteria for quality based more squarely upon pedagogic considerations. The final section elaborates upon the crisis of reform in education and training exemplified within the case study college.

The potential of a reflective practitioner model of teaching

A significant advantage to FE lecturers of the notion of the reflective practitioner is that it provides a conceptual framework within which the complexities, tensions and contradictions of their work can be explored, and at the same time it provides a reference point against which the intrinsic value of their practice can be judged. Carr (1992, p.251) argues that only the reflective teacher can adequately engage with the moral and evaluative roots and the complexity of educational discourse. To reconstruct the lecturer as a reflective practitioner draws attention to the relationship of the lecturer with the range of types and levels of activity which constitute his or her own practice, and to the barriers to the implementation of policy-driven change. The potential for lecturers to inform and influence policy, and the process by which lecturers make considered responses to political, cultural and technological change, and devise considered strategies to contain or exploit both intended and unintended consequences, are also key issues which are given prominence within a reflective practice model of teaching.

One major gain of such a perspective is that it achieves a defensible conception of educational theory, which resonates with Pring's (1978) definition of theory as 'critical and systematic reflection on practice', and meets his earlier criticism of educational theory, that it is 'generally divorced from educational practice' (Pring 1976, p.19). Another major gain of this approach is that it can link teaching in FE with an important and influential body of literature, providing a theoretical and conceptual orientation which has the capacity to inform, improve and, perhaps most important at the present time, value lecturers' own reflective practice against the impositions of market-based policies at national and institutional level.

Further implications of the reflective practitioner model for theory are pointed up by Griffiths and Tann (1991):

...reflective teaching requires that public theories are translated into personal ones and vice versa, unless teachers are going to allow themselves to be turned into low-level operatives, content with carrying out their tasks more and more efficiently, while remaining blind to larger issues of the underlying purposes and results of schooling. (p.100)

Reflective practice entails that the lecturer carries out his or her work towards ethical ends, which may characteristically be expressed by them altruistically. The work, no matter how varied, how menial in parts, is underpinned by a notion of educational worth.

Schratz (1993a; 1993b) has reported gains in the development of a culture of self-evaluation and personnel development across disciplines through an action research programme promoting a model of reflection-in-action within a higher education institution. Elliott (1989), Adler (1993) and Merryfield (1993) have similarly highlighted the advantages of focusing on reflection as a critical component in teacher education.

Singh (1994) argues that the reflective practice model has presaged a broadening consensus as to the desirability of developing, in school pupils, critical thinking skills – this approach being underpinned, he suggests, by the settlement of notions of cultural pluralism within a framework of universal moral principles.

In addition to the benefits at the level of practice, there are significant gains at the level of theory to a reflective practitioner model. Constructing reflective practice as an epistemology, rather than a methodology, frees it from the theoretical straitjacket of any single research tradition and opens up the possibility of exploring practice from a variety of perspectives. Reflective practice has been closely associated in the literature with the action research tradition, but such an association may not have been helpful. Action research has been soundly criticised for conceptual *naïveté*, inadequate theory formulation, and a demonstrable failure to realise its potential to bring about significant change (see e.g. Adelman 1989, pp.177–8).

Skilbeck (1983), on the other hand, has noted the benefits for 'teachers in school, educational advisers and academics who are carrying forward a general style of reflective inquiry of which Stenhouse is the principal luminary' (p.18). In their study of teacher-researchers on a university course, Vulliamy and Webb (1992) found 'that the in-depth reflection on practice, promoted on the course by case study and action research, often made a major contribution to participants' professional development and led to changes in policy and practice for which they were responsible' (p.43).

It is of critical importance to a teacher education agenda for the incorporated FE sector that the inter-relationship, noted in this study, between lecturer pedagogy, education policy and managerialist HRM strategies, is fully explored in order to question what Gore (1993) calls the 'regime of pedagogy', which assumes that such issues are unproblematic (p.144). It is here argued that only by exhorting trainee lecturers critically to examine their practice – to engage in reflective practice as a political act directed towards change and improvement – that the damaging effects of policy and managerialist practice, noted in this study at the level of practical action within the FE sector, might be ameliorated.

The tension between the two central themes in this study – the market in education and lecturers' reflective practice – has pointed up an important policy issue. Attempts by college managers to impose a particular type of business ethic within the college appear to have been resisted by lecturers in this case study. The data show that the lecturers are not resistant to business methods and practices *per se*; on the contrary, on issues such as appraisal, the use of external performance indicators and in relation to the autonomy brought about by incorporation, lecturers can, in many cases, see clear advantages of such initiatives. It is clear, however, that lecturers actively evaluate new developments and changes on their merits. New initiatives are seldom pre-judged, but are addressed in relation to their perceived benefits for the students. Where, for example, external performance indicators are perceived to assist lecturers in developing and improving their practice or encourage them to reflect upon and review the effectiveness of their teaching, they are welcomed. Lecturers have clear and shared priorities which are seldom far from the surface. These priorities acted as a benchmark, against which both education policy and the practices and procedures of senior managers were measured. Crucially, even where lecturers are sympathetic to the difficulties faced by senior managers dealing with incorporation or where they can see advantages with formalised procedures, they remain very resistant to such procedures. It appears that it is the manner and style of implementation, rather than the initiatives themselves, that provoke the hostility and antagonism which characterise relations between lecturers and managers. If the suggestion that these lecturers are a critical factor in the transmission of policy at the level of teaching and learning is more generally true, this holds some significance for those who wish to explore the conditions under which policy for the sector may be successfully implemented.

Future study may need to assess how far policymakers may underestimate the extent to which their policies provoke resistance, especially if they fail to understand the degree to which lecturers' resistance is circumscribed by their cultural and ideological assumptions and dispositions. Managers, too, may underplay these factors and may fail accurately to 'read' the real potential, illustrated within this study, for changing practice and procedures in their colleges. It is of major importance to recognise that policymakers and managers alike may reap practical benefits by questioning the logic of their assumptions with regard to lecturers' practice.

If, as this study suggests, lecturers are, potentially and in practice, open to the benefits of innovation, it is in managers' interest actively to explore the extent to which, and under what conditions, lecturers are prepared to review and amend their practice. By the same token, it seems likely to be counter-productive if managers set up mechanistic and system-serving procedures which lecturers regard as against their own and their students' best interests. Time and again lecturers reported that the managers in this college failed to communicate their intentions or signal their policies to staff. The effect of this is that dialogue seldom occurs, and, as a consequence, for the most part lecturers feel alienated and disempowered.

Short-term resolution of the cultural tensions highlighted in this study may well be difficult. It is suggested that the FE college is a 'site of struggle' (Althusser 1971) in which competing ideologies are fought out for dominance. In practice, it seems that both co-exist, giving rise to an on-going state of mutual hostility, characterised by miscommunication, noncompliance, misunderstanding of practice and lack of support. The tensions and dilemmas which are reflected in the data confirm the analysis of Ball and Bowe (1991), which suggests that a management strategy of market-led planning in educational institutions will generate value changes which become polarised into two cross-cutting oppositions: 'One is concerned with institutional goals and priorities, placing "educating" students above and against marketing, while the other is related to organisational control and managing, which are considerations that are set above and against consulting' (p.27).

Their model, highlighting conflicting forces within education, is confirmed by the evidence of the lecturers' accounts. An adapted model for FE is therefore proposed (Figure 7.1) upon which future research might build. It is beyond the scope of this study to propose comprehensive national or organisational policy solutions to tensions that may well be played out in FE

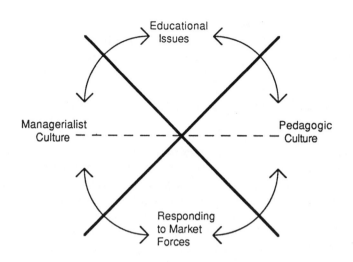

Figure 7.1 Tensions and dilemmas in the incorporated FE sector (with an acknowledgement to Ball and Bowe 1991, p.27)

colleges and other educational institutions. It is a matter for further investigation as to the extent to which the tensions and themes identified in this study are typical or indicative of situations elsewhere. Anecdotal evidence suggests that the phenomenon of a clash of culture between college managers and lecturers is not new, but also that the consequences have been more direct, and more readily apparent, following incorporation. This is a view which is supported both by the myriad internal college disputes, and extensive nationwide union action, following the imposition of new contracts and conditions of service for FE lecturing staff.

Implications for college managers

As argued elsewhere (Elliott and Hall 1994, pp.3–4) and as shown in this study, the FE sector is being forced by external pressure from a service to a business orientation, which is having an impact upon management strategies and styles. Incorporation can be seen both as a consequence and a development of this trend and it has been suggested that significant responses by college managers to the newly incorporated status of their colleges have been the introduction of Human Resource Management strategies, and formal quality assurance systems, which help them meet the system demands of incorporation, and at the same time undermine and help to bring about the marginalisation of a pedagogic orientation at both strategic and operational levels.

The evidence of the mismatch, from the point of view of the lecturers in this study, between their pedagogic culture and the managerialist culture of the senior college managers is important. FE colleges have been urged to adopt a more businesslike approach to the conduct of their operations. Management literature (e.g. Peters and Waterman 1982) in use in recent years at the Staff College in the management development of college managers, proposes the development and achievement of organisational excellence through a focus upon 'customer service'. The NVQs in Customer Service are being introduced for lecturing staff in some English FE colleges, including the case study college. However, the evidence of this study points to a significant barrier to the implementation of such business-derived strategies. Without adapting such initiatives so that they support or correspond with the lecturers' pedagogic orientation, and without effective communication of the purpose and benefits of such initiatives, they seem doomed to failure (McBean 1994). It seems more than possible that lecturers' adaptations made in relation to the new initiatives, student-centred approaches and orientation towards improving the learning experience for their students, have been confused by senior college managers for 'customer service'. This slippage appears to have occurred in a pre-incorporation study by Frain (1993) of the Liverpool FE college where he was principal, where it is stated:

> It is easy to discern the quality, reliability and loyalty in client relationships...replicated in the attitudes of staff to so many of the College's students and client organizations. Management had felt that one of its primary tasks was to further foster the client-led attitude already internalized by many staff. (p.183)

If the senior managers in the case study college are making this kind of assumption, then the need for them to recognise the existence of competing cultures becomes apparent and urgent.

It is doubtful, however, whether a simple change of strategy would be sufficient to persuade lecturing staff to embrace managerialist policies, particularly those which centre around Human Resource Management and quality assurance procedures, which determine and potentially limit the lecturers' ability to carry out their pedagogical role in relation to their students. The depth and extent of difference between the two cultures evidenced in this study suggests that it is only by significantly modifying such managerialist approaches that college managers can turn resistance into co-operation and collaboration.

The extent to which most lecturers in the study have a sophisticated appreciation of the system demands of incorporation appreciate the difficulty and responsibility of the management role, and support initiatives such as appraisal, exposes as a myth the view, promulgated by the CEF, that lecturers are backward-looking and resistant to change. Whilst lecturers are not powerless to act within the college, they are, as a matter of policy, disempowered in relation to the key decision-making processes. Staff consultation is rare, and when it does occur, bears the hallmark of tokenism. The consistent view of the lecturing staff is that senior management are out of touch; indeed it has been seen that a recurring theme within the data has to do with the perceived distance between the activities and concerns of college managers and those of lecturers who are primarily concerned with teaching students.

One way forward would be for colleges to eschew managerialist strategies in favour of a strategy of empowerment of their lecturing staff. Central to this notion is a view of staff which is diametrically opposed to that which underlies Human Resource Management models. Empowerment involves a management commitment to the provision of staff development opportunities for lecturers in the processes and systems which would enable them to carry out both lower and higher level decision-making within the institution. Lecturers, thus equipped, could be given control over the resourcing and staffing requirements of their areas, albeit within an allotted budget. Other areas, such as marketing, recruitment, student services, could be organised centrally or devolved as a matter of college policy. It is the resourcing decision, and the key issues to do with the selection and control of the curriculum, which need to be prioritised for devolution to individual lecturers and to the smallest unit of operational activity within the college structure, the course team. The view that lecturers, as those closest to the area of curriculum operations, are in the best position to take decisions affecting that area is consistent with some influential management thinking (e.g. Peters 1989) that 'de-layering' is an effective way of increasing organisational efficiency and effectiveness.

One form of empowerment which might have potential for bridging cultural differences between college managers and lecturers would be the use of quality assurance systems which are grounded in the everyday practice of lecturers. The present study suggests that review and evaluation models being developed prior to incorporation (Miller and Innis 1990) hold most potential for satisfying criteria which lecturers hold as important: straightforward, related to teaching, consistent with existing practice in curriculum review and evaluation, and legitimated at the point of delivery, that is, involving student representation.

An important principle of empowerment, and a reason why it is resisted by managers, is that it involves both letting go of power from the centre and, at the same time, continuing to take overall responsibility for the actions of junior staff (Gretton 1995, p.22). Managers baulk at the prospect of 'losing control' in this way. In fact the reverse becomes possible, since a situation where accountability is bottom-up and information flows from the top down is changed to one where a two-way direction of accountability and information occurs. Managers are accountable for putting in place appropriate staff development programmes to enable staff to develop the necessary management skills, whilst staff are responsible for making sure that managers are kept fully briefed as to the outcomes of decisions taken on the ground, within the lecturer's remit, which require addressing at a higher or wider level within the organisation.

Central to this model, however, is agreement upon, or at least a mutual recognition of what might count as, legitimate work for lecturing staff. The ongoing introduction of formal appraisal systems for lecturers in FE colleges has not led to any systematic attempt to categorise and describe what lecturers do. Clearly appraisal is going to be problematic in circumstances where there is ambiguity, disagreement or ignorance about what does and should constitute legitimate, effective and purposeful activity for lecturers. As Day and Pennington (1993) have pointed out, in the context of teacher staff development, efficiency and effectiveness demand that 'it is vital that key commitments, qualities, knowledge, skills and tasks of teachers are identified' (p.251).

There are, therefore, pressing and highly pertinent operational and strategic advantages for college managers identifying and understanding what lecturers do. Whilst colleges may vary in their commitment to the personal development of their lecturing staff, if there is an implementation gap between what managers expect lecturers to do, what lecturers feel they should do, and what they do do, it would be as well for both parties to be aware of it.

Managers could, it is argued, effectively discharge their responsibility to manage change by adopting a reflective practice perspective, which has the potential to turn managers away from managerialist approaches towards 'a clearer theory of reflective management' (Lomas 1993, p.76). Duignan (1989, p.78) similarly stresses the benefits of reflective practice for educational managers and other practitioners who wish to engage in successful management of change. There are also benefits of the model for learning support for school managers (Wallace 1991, p.35), especially in facilitating the making of connections between theory and practice.

In the conclusion to a case study of a Liverpool college cited earlier, Frain (1993) foresees that colleges which will flourish under incorporation will be those which take decisive action: 'The organizations that survive and prosper in the face of increasing pressure to innovate will possess nimble leadership and will establish an organization-wide creative and innovative culture' (p.191). To the extent that this prescription for success ignores the need for college managers to recognise *existing* lecturer cultures which are oppositional to those carried by managers, it will fail.

As this study has shown, there is, within the lecturing force, a degree of commonality with managers on a range of issues –

such as the need for effective external and internal evaluation of practice – fundamental to the successful management of change. What the study has not tested is the extent to which college managers would be prepared to forego managerialist approaches in order to accommodate lecturers' priorities as a vehicle for further change and reform. It is unlikely, given the competing priorities of managerialist and pedagogic cultures, that significant progress will be made without considerable accommodations on both sides. The evidence of this study is that the lecturers, whilst having a deep-seated commitment to pedagogic values, have endorsed a number of new initiatives where they have identified benefits for themselves or their students. What appears to be missing, therefore, is a response from the managers which is communicated effectively to all other staff.

The penetration and persistence of a pedagogic work culture, which is diametrically opposed to many elements of the managerialist culture which may be found within an FE college, must at least be recognised and then accommodated within any strategy for the establishment of a new adaptive culture for the 21st century. Not only must college managers share their responsibility for changing the culture, as Frain notes (1993, p.192), but they must also recognise the existence and legitimacy of existing cultures which have supported and propelled the FE sector into the prominent and successful position which is fully recognised and celebrated in the text of the 1991 FE White Paper (DES 1991).

Qualitative research methods and management studies

This section explores some implications of the study for management studies and the development of college managers. As noted elsewhere (Elliott and Crossley 1994), external pressures following incorporation have made it more likely that college managers will seek out quantitative data in order to meet performance indicators and to satisfy funding criteria. Such a trend needs to be counter-balanced by a concern with the consequences of policy decisions in practice, at the level of educational action, and that methodologies inspired by principles of qualitative research, 'in particular case study and practitioner research – are ideally suited to such a task' (p.188). Given the climate of change in the FE sector, grounded theory approaches would appear to have much potential for managers and others wishing to follow Stenhouse (1978) in exploring the implications of policy at the level of action, thus engaging with the macro as well as the micro context. Indeed: 'The implication that educational policy at the national level determines a particular pattern or mode of decision-making throughout an institution should be resisted. To do so will involve managers, researchers, and others who wish to know, seeking out different understandings and differing practices within educational institutions' (Elliott 1993, p.39).

The culture gap which is held to exist between managers and lecturers may, in part, be a consequence of the neglect of qualitative information on the part of college managers. For example, an understanding of the real and deeply-held orientation to a student-centred pedagogy, evidenced amongst all the lecturers in this study, might point college managers towards a more collegial mode of college organisation, within which such concerns might not only be expressed, but, more positively incorporated in the fabric of college organisational systems.

In the present context of rapid change which characterises the FE sector, it remains essential that policy and managerial decisions are accompanied by 'effective monitoring and feedback' (Stenhouse 1978, p.29) in order to assess the impact of short- and medium-term strategic planning. It is also vital that educational action, as the carrying out of the consequences of decisions in practice, is accompanied by 'moment to moment judgement' (p.29) in order that the effects of new policy can be effectively evaluated to ensure the quality of educational experience.

In examining the potential contribution of qualitative research and evaluation for management information, it is important to be clear about the implications of the rise, noted earlier, of the 'quality and accountability' movement in the post-compulsory sector. This movement is wedded to analyses which are based almost exclusively upon quantitative data. If managers, therefore, wish to question such analyses, it becomes necessary to present alternative data grounded in the distinctive characteristics of each institution. The reason for this is that the data collected and analysed using quantitative methodologies are typically of such a simplistic nature that there is, in fact, little room for manoeuvre on interpretation of the data itself.

Quantitative research – which is broad brush, which focuses on macro issues, which is carried out by external research staff, which is designed to investigate the existence of evidence in relation to preset indicators, which does not concern itself with the singular characteristics of institutions, their environments, or their practices – tends to undervalue the practitioner as a resource and, in so doing, undervalues the importance of the pedagogic process itself. Current debates on 'quality' in education are heavily informed by the quantitative tradition, and hence the emphasis is upon measurable and observable outcomes of an education system which, many would argue, is in the process of being hijacked by accountants and business managers whose profit – loss, efficiency-led ideology is occupying every corner of compulsory and post-compulsory education.

Against this background, it is here argued that for the education manager there is much to be gained from increased attention to qualitative research strategies, and in particular those that support and encourage practitioner research, and which focus upon the quality of the curriculum offered to students (Kershaw 1994). Managers, by virtue of their position in the organisational structure, will be in possession of a wealth of data in the form of reported information, both documentary and oral, as well as a vast store of data arising from everyday experience, knowledge and understanding. These data will be in many ways unique both to the individual and to the institution. The research strategy which stands to maximise the use of such data is practitioner research, which is here used in the sense suggested by Webb of a catch-all term to refer to 'case-study research and evaluation and action research undertaken by teachers, advisers, lecturers and others who work within the education system' (Webb 1990, p.1).

Such research can inform the learning and teaching process and is required as a counter-balance to the quantitative data which are collected by external players (e.g. FEFC, TECs, Governors) and which serve *their* needs (Elliott 1996). The point about the relative value of these two research models for practitioners is well put by Webb (1990): '...traditional research, pursued from the vantage point of specialists and couched in their terms, has been rejected by practising teachers as of little use in assisting them to analyse classroom situations and in devising solutions to practical problems' (p.3). On the other hand, '...research into the processes of teaching and learning and/or the factors which directly affect these processes...employs methods of enquiry, ways of presenting findings and publication outlets that are eclectic, pragmatic and readily accessible to teachers' (p.3).

Perhaps an even more important benefit for managers accruing from the use of qualitative research methods is the potential they offer for fostering a closer interrelationship between theory and practice. There are strong antecedents for such a claim in the work of Glaser and Strauss (1967), in that inherent in their notion of 'grounded theory' is the idea that theory is generated from data gathered through participant research rather than imposed externally upon the data by researchers who are coming from – both literally and epistemologically – outside the educational institution.

Atkinson and Delamont (1985) have rightly pointed out that much case study research in education has failed to make illuminative use of case studies in other contexts outside of education. They advocate the development of comparative perspectives in order to generate formal concepts, that is, 'abstract, ideal-typical, notions which characterise features, problems and issues which may be common to a range of different concrete settings' (p.40). This approach is consistent with the call for a more adventurous and eclectic approach to policy studies made by Ball and Shilling (1994). The aim of such work would be to move beyond what Hurst (1987) calls 'the Western ethnocentrism and parochialism which so disfigures most writing about education...(in order to tap)...the quiddity, the uniqueness of particular cultures, contexts and personalities – which qualitative research is specifically configured to explore' (p.72).

It is precisely this model of practitioner research which is here being advocated for educational managers. It has been emphasised throughout this study that post-compulsory education is currently being dominated by a managerial business ethic, led by market forces, which is influencing how the sector is evaluated, and how it is internally managed. The privatisation of formerly public sector HE and FE institutions is the most visible manifestation of the market forces movement in education. There is thus an inescapable logic which invites comparative analysis between educational institutions and business institutions. Such an analysis will point-up the extent of the hegemonic imposition of the one culture upon the other, and the implications for all concerned of such an imposition. The limitations of such moves have been well documented in the context of international transfer (Crossley 1984), but remain less visible when operational between sectors within one state. A careful evaluation of processes and outcomes will be necessary if educational managers are to understand the nature of the forces at work in the transfer of working practices between different work contexts and, by understanding, control or resist them. The resulting analysis will be all the stronger if it can be supported by comparative studies with other service and business institutions. The use of multiple comparison groups, as described by Glaser and Strauss (1966), to compare and contrast educational organisations with other organisations, has much potential for, and has been little used in, published educational research.

One invaluable area of research which such a methodology could explore has to do with policy effects. Finch has shown that qualitative research is undervalued in the formulation of public policy. However, the present study confirms Finch's view that qualitative research can illuminate whether policy initiatives lead to substantive or illusory change, what the unintended consequences are, and highlight the internal contradictions often present in policy formulation and implementation (Finch 1988, pp.188–190). One policy initiative which it is vital should be explored and evaluated by managers is the proposed imposition by college managers of the CEF changes in lecturers' conditions of service. The push towards greater efficiency in the FE sector during the 1980s has led to general acceptance by senior college managers of an orthodoxy which places high value upon minimum teacher-class contact, maximum occupancy of space, reduced remission in relation to support roles for full-time lecturers and greater utilisation of short-term contracts and of part-time lecturers. Management courses for FE managers are promoting this orthodoxy on a wide scale. This perspective is continually re-established by colleges' own performance indicators, which are strong on efficiency criteria, and by the introduction of performance-related pay. It has been further reinforced by the three-stage 'entry – on programme –

exit' funding model in use by the FEFC. Yet seemingly little account is taken of the experienced and unanticipated effects of these measures upon the processes of learning and teaching in colleges.

Lecturers widely regard the single-minded pursuit of efficiency through performance indicators as contrary to their students' and their own best interests, and as incompatible with their own conceptions of quality. The widespread result has been a general withdrawal of 'goodwill'. In some cases, this has led to wholesale abuse of internal policies and procedures, where lecturers play the system and obstruct, as far as is within their power, any attempt to further thin resources. Comparative studies, and studies which make use of multiple comparison groups, which can find parallels in other public sector organisations (hospitals, local authorities, subsidised arts organisations), could demonstrate associations, processes and typifications which together can form what Rock (1979, p.50) calls 'a grammar which is intended to provide working recipes for an understanding of the abstract properties of social life'. There is thus a strong argument for a network whereby managers can access case records and findings made in other educational settings in order to evaluate the effects of the many innovations taking place in the post-compulsory sector. As Crossley and Vulliamy (1984) point out:

> Through their concern with the everyday practices of teachers and students, case study methods are well placed to identify important constraints on innovation, which may not be apparent to policy-makers who necessarily lack a detailed understanding of the local context in which innovations are being attempted. (p.199)

There is a widely recognised need for managers in the post-compulsory sector who can more effectively manage innovation, adaptation and change. Qualitative research methods can provide the educational manager with a highly effective management tool that is highly sensitive to the perspectives of those directly involved in the teaching and learning process. Improving managers' understanding of policy and practice will be vital in helping them to manage the process of change successfully, and to avoid what could become a real, but hidden, cycle of decline.

The crisis of reform

This final section attempts to draw the threads of this study together and to locate the contradictions being played out within the college within the wider crisis of reform of education and training in England. The unceasing government-led drive towards a radical right-wing orientation within education has brought with it a new orthodoxy which is legitimated and supported by a new vocabulary. The orthodoxy is one of transience and contingency. There is no place within such a vision for traditional values of the right or the left. Instead, the market decides, *caveat emptor*. Education is a quasi-market, since most who participate do not pay directly for it, but it is no less market-led for that. For many, education has become a service industry whose product is conceptualised as a commodity. Choice, customer focus and charter marks are accessories of the market-place and education has become adorned with them.

It is within this context that the lecturers and managers in this study worked out their separate agendas. Both, in a sense, are victims of a system which is determined by government interventionism. Yet at the same time, the possibilities of varying responses and proactive strategies are clearly indicated within the data. The market paradigm offers, at one and the same time, constraint and opportunity. However, these two dimensions do not divide simplistically along a line between managers and managed. Lecturers respond in both positive and negative ways to the unfolding manifestations of the market in their college. As for the managers, they seem to be more closely bound by the chaotic, but manipulative, imperatives which they face as business managers who appear to be willing, but unprepared, victims of incorporation.

The crisis of reform in the college is deep-seated, having both cultural and political manifestations. The resulting disorder becomes a metaphor for the collisions between rationalistic managerialism and negotiated collegiality. Pfeffer and Salancik (1978) characterise an organisation as 'a coalition of groups and interests, each attempting to obtain something from the collectivity by interacting with others, and each with its own preferences and objectives' (p.36). To the extent that this notion conjures up a picture of competing rationalities and unintended consequences, it strikes many chords in relation to the clearly differing priorities of lecturers and managers. However, the interests, preferences and objectives of all participants in the incorporated FE sector need to be understood and interpreted within the context of political influence and control. By adopting the rules of competition within a market-place, those within the institution are, arguably, attempting to preserve a learning and teaching environment which they value. Increasingly, however, the rules of discourse within the college make it more and more difficult for lecturers to maintain continuity in prioritising pedagogy over the imperatives of the market. Appealing to a moral principle or an educational aim becomes increasingly futile since debates with senior managers can only be conducted in relation to the 'bottom line'.

The vigour with which college managers embraced the market paradigm suggests that, for them, the opportunities of incorporation were long overdue. In dealing with Human Resource Management issues during the 1980s, managers felt that their hands were tied in that they were subject to the authority of the LEA and thereby unwilling parties to the Silver Book agreement which guaranteed a range of entitlements, including a specified national maximum number of teaching contact hours. During the period immediately leading up to incorporation day itself, managers were locked in dispute with lecturers – with strike action over conditions of service threatening to dampen the celebrations which were planned. Subsequently, the power, influence and membership of the main college lecturer union have declined dramatically. The lecturers' so-called 'professional contract', local pay bargaining and performance-related pay are well-established throughout the sector. The discourse of the marketeer has become an orthodoxy with customer service, total quality and performance indicators maintaining a high profile.

What is to be done? By engaging in a technocratic discourse, both lecturers and managers have become locked into a cycle of tension, contradiction and decline, just as all colleges in the sector have become competitors in a game in which the losers are taken over by the winners. The market demands that colleges compete with each other to win students in order to demonstrate ever increasing efficiency gains. But this market is silent as to the needs of students. Whilst the government claims to be increasing participation through the implementation of its current policies, there are few signals from opposition parties or from within the sector itself as to alternative strategies. No-one can imagine dismantling the quasi-market that has been created and putting in place committed government of post-compulsory education. West (1996), writing about the schools sector, argues for a locally accountable democratic model of educational policy:

> ...the problems of modern society can only be resolved by the fostering of new civic partnerships: the involvement of education's stakeholders. The political voice and skills of governing bodies and local communities are important elements in this: the only elements at present perhaps that can lift schools out of the sterile concentration of administration. and technique: there is in other words a need for the concept of self-management to extend to that of self-governance and co-governance, for without political voice and participation, at the local level the skills of government could so easily be replaced by a tier of technocrats – the accessories of hegemony. We have to begin again in building the democratic process and in unearthing civic awareness from traditional assumptions, paternalism and market silences. (p.92)

The political context of further education is one of hegemonic influence and control, where debate is constrained within a technocratic market discourse, to the point where many lecturers are experiencing the fundamental contradiction of educational practice: 'the experience of holding educational values, and the experience of their negation' (Whitehead 1989, p.44). There would appear to be only a single way forward, and that is to find strategies which replace the dominant discourse with one which is predicated upon collaboration rather than competition. Whether or not this is possible within the current political climate is open to debate. There is an emerging swing away from conflict to consensus models in education (Lawton 1992; Hall and Wallace 1993; Macbeth, McCreath and Aitchinson, Eds. 1995; Bridges and Husbands, Eds. 1996). Whether this trend can be sustained, and have the force to steer a direction through the crisis of reform, is another matter.

References

Adelman, C. (1989) 'The practical ethic takes priority over methodology.' In W. Carr (ed) *Quality in Teaching: Arguments for a Reflective Profession*. Lewes: The Falmer Press.

Adler, S. (1993) 'Teacher education: research as reflective practice.' *Teacher and Teacher Education 9*, 2, 159–167.

Althusser, L. (1971) 'Ideology and ideological state apparatuses.' In *Lenin and Philosophy and Other Essays*. London: New Left Books.

Altrichter, H. and Posch, P. (1989) 'Does the "grounded theory" approach offer a guiding paradigm for teacher research?' *Cambridge Journal of Education 19*, 1, 21–31.

Apple, M. (1986) *Teachers and Texts: A Political Economy of Class and Gender Relations in Education*. London: Routledge and Kegan Paul.

Apple, M. (1989) 'Critical introduction: ideology and the state in educational policy.' In R. Dale (1989) *The State and Education Policy*. Milton Keynes: Open University Press.

Ashworth, P. (1992) 'Being competent and having "competencies".' *Journal of Further and Higher Education 16*, 3, 8–17.

Astuto, T. and Clark, D. (1986) 'Achieving effective schools.' In E. Hoyle and A. McMahon (eds) *World Yearbook of Education 1986: The Management of Schools*. London: Kogan Page.

Atkinson, P. and Delamont, S. (1985) 'Bread and dreams or bread and circuses? A critique of "case study" research in education.' In M. Shipman (ed) *Educational Research*. Lewes: The Falmer Press.

Audit Commission (1985) *Obtaining Better Value from Further Education*. London: HMSO.

Avis, J. (1994) 'Teacher professionalism: one more time,' *Educational Review 46*, 1, 63–72.

Ayres, D. (1990) 'Deskilling teacher assessment in GCSE?' *Forum 33*, 1, 20–22.

Baker, K. (1989) Speech to the Association of Colleges of Further and Higher Education (ACFHE) February 15.

Ball, S. (1993a) 'Education policy, power relations and teachers' work.' *British Journal of Educational Studies 41*, 2, 106–121.

Ball, S. (1993b) 'Education markets, choice and social class: the market as a class strategy in the UK and the USA.' *British Journal of Sociology of Education 14*, 1, 3–19.

Ball, S. and Bowe, R. (1991) 'Micropolitics of radical change: budgets, management and control in British schools.' In J. Blase. *The Politics of Life in Schools*. London: Sage.

Ball, S. and Shilling, C. (1994) 'Guest editorial: at the cross-roads: education policy studies.' *British Journal of Educational Studies 42*, 1, 1–5.

Becher, T. and Kogan, M. (1992 2nd Edn) *Process and Structure in Higher Education*. London: Routledge.

Becker, H. (1958) 'Problems of inference and proof in participant observation.' *American Sociological Review 23*, 652–660.

Becker, H. (1971) 'Comment.' In M. Wax, S. Diamond and F. Gearing (eds) *Anthropological Perspectives upon Education*. New York: Basic Books.

Becker, H., Geer, B., Hughes, E. and Strauss, A. (1961) *Boys in White: Student Culture in Medical School*. Chicago: University of Chicago Press.

Belbin, R. (1981) *Management Teams: Why they Succeed or Fail*. Oxford: Butterworth-Heinemann.

Bennett, N., Crawford, M. and Riches, C. (eds) (1992) *Managing Change in Education*. London: Paul Chapman/Open University Press.

Bines, H. (1992) 'Freedom, inequality and the market in further and higher education, review symposium.' *British Journal of Sociology of Education 13*, 1, 113–116.

Blase, J. (1991) 'The micropolitical perspective.' In J. Blase (ed) *The Politics of Life in Schools*. London: Sage.

Bogdan, R. and Biklen, S. (2nd Edn 1992) *Qualitative Research for Education*. Boston: Allyn and Bacon.

Boswell, T. (1994) Speech to the Association for Colleges in London, Post-16 Current Awareness Bulletin Alerting Service, April, Coventry: NCET.

Bottery, M. (1992) *The Ethics of Educational Management: Personal, Social and Political Perspectives on School Organisation.* London: Cassell.

Bowe, R. and Ball, S. with Gold, A. (1992) *Reforming Education and Changing Schools.* London: Routledge.

Boyatzis, R. (1982) *The Competent Manager.* New York: John Wiley.

Bridges, D. and Husbands, C. (1996) *Consorting and Collaborating in the Education Marketplace.* London: The Falmer Press.

British Standards Institution (BSI) (1987) *BS 5750: Part 1. Specification for Design, Development, Production, Installation and Servicing.* London: BSI.

Brook, L. (1970, 2nd Edn.) 'Further what?' In D. Rubinstein and C. Stoneman (eds) *Education for Democracy.* Harmondsworth: Penguin.

Burgess, R. (1984) *In the Field.* London: Allen and Unwin.

Burrell, G. and Morgan, G. (1979) *Sociological Paradigms and Organisational Analysis.* London: Heinemann.

Carr, D. (1992) 'Practical enquiry, values and the problem of educational theory.' *Oxford Review of Education 18*, 3, 241–251.

Carr, D. (1993) 'Questions of competence.' *British Journal of Educational Studies 41*, 3, 253–271.

Carr, D. (1994) 'Educational enquiry and professional knowledge: towards a Copernican revolution.' *Educational Studies 20*, 1, 33–52.

Carr, W. (1987) 'What is an educational practice?' *Journal of Philosophy of Education 21*, 2, 163–175.

Carr, W. and Kemmis, S. (1986) *Becoming Critical: Education, Knowledge and Action Research.* London: The Falmer Press.

Chitty, C. (1989) *Towards a New Education System: The Victory of the New Right?* London: Falmer Press.

Chomsky, N. (1971) *Chomsky: Selected Readings.* Edited by J. Allen and P. Van Buren. Oxford: Oxford University Press.

Chown, A. (1992) 'TDLB standards in FE.' *Journal of Further and Higher Education 16*, 3, 52–59.

Chown, A. and Last, J. (1993) 'Can the NCVQ model be used for teacher training?' *Journal of Further and Higher Education 17*, 2, 15–26.

Cohen, M. and March, J. (1974) 'Leadership and ambiguity: the American college president.' In T. Bush (ed 1989) *Managing Education: Theory and Practice*. Milton Keynes: Open University Press.

College Employers' Forum (1993) *Draft Contract of Employment for Academic Staff Appointed or Promoted After 1st April 1993*. London: Norton Rose.

Collins, N. (1993) NVQ Customer Service Award at Level 3. Information Sheet presented to managers of the case study college.

Crossley, M. (1984) 'Strategies for curriculum change and the question of international transfer.' *Journal of Curriculum Studies 16*, 1, 75–88.

Crossley, M. and Vulliamy, G. (1984) 'Case study research methods and comparative education.' *Comparative Education 20*, 2, 193–207.

Cuthbert, R. (1988) *Going Corporate*. Bristol: The Further Education Staff College.

Dale, R. (1989) *The State and Education Policy*. Milton Keynes: Open University Press.

Darling-Hammond, L. (1989) 'Accountability for professional practice.' *Teachers' College Record 91*, 1, 59–79.

Day, C. and Pennington, A. (1993) 'Conceptualising professional development planning: a multidimensional model.' *International Analysis of Teacher Education, Journal of Education for Teaching, Papers One*. Oxford: Carfax.

Deal, T. and Kennedy, A. (1982) *Corporate Cultures*. Reading, Mass: Addison-Wesley.

Dean, C. (1993) 'Academics attack market madness.' *Times Educational Supplement*. September 10, p.2.

Dennison, W. and Shenton, K. (1990) 'Training professional leaders: the new school managers.' *Oxford Review of Education 16*, 3, 311–320.

Department of Education and Science (1987) *Managing Colleges Efficiently*. London: HMSO.

Department of Education and Science (1988a) *Education Reform Act*. London: HMSO.

Department of Education and Science (1988b) *Circular 9/88.* London HMSO.

Department of Education and Science (1991) *Education and Training for the 21st Century.* DES/ED/Welsh Office Cm 1536 Vols 1 and 2. London: HMSO.

Department of Education and Science (1992) *Further and Higher Education Act.* London: HMSO.

Deville, H. (1987) 'Vocational qualifications.' *Education Today 37,* 4, 9–13.

Dewey, J. (1970 [1929]) 'The sources of a science of education. In M. Skilbeck (ed) *John Dewey.* London: Collier-Macmillan.

Dewey, J. (1933 Revised Edn) *How We Think: A Restatement of the Relation of Reflective Thinking to the Educative Process.* Boston: D C Heath and Co.

Duignan, P. (1989) 'Reflective management: the key to quality leadership.' In C. Riches and C. Morgan (eds) *Human Resource Management in Education.* Milton Keynes: Open University Press.

Eisner, E. (1967) 'Educational objectives: help or hindrance?' In D. Hamilton, D. Jenkins, C. King, B. MacDonald and M. Parlett (eds 1977) *Beyond the Numbers Game: A Reader in Educational Evaluation.* London: Macmillan.

Eisner, E. (1969) 'Instructional and expressive objectives.' In D. Hamilton, D. Jenkins, C. King, B. MacDonald and M. Parlett (eds) (1977) *Beyond the Numbers Game: A Reader in Educational Evaluation.* London: Macmillan.

Elliott, G. (1993) 'Whose quality is it anyway?' *Quality Assurance in Education 1,* 1, 34–40.

Elliott, G. (1996) 'Why is research invisible in further education?' *British Educational Research Journal 22,* 1, 101–111.

Elliott, G. and Crossley, M. (1994) 'Qualitative research, educational management and the incorporation of the further education sector.' *Educational Management and Administration 22,* 3, 188–197.

Elliott, G. and Hall, V. (1994) 'FE Inc – business orientation in further education and the introduction of human resource management.' *School Organisation 14,* 1, 3–10.

Elliott, J. (1989) 'Educational theory and the professional learning of teachers: an overview.' *Cambridge Journal of Education 19,* 1, 81–101.

Elliott, J. (1991) 'A model of professionalism and its implications for teacher education.' *British Educational Research Journal 17*, 4, 309–318.

Ellis, P. and Gorringe, R. (1989) 'Continuing education and training through competence-based vocational qualifications.' *Educational and Training Technology International 26*, 1, 7–13.

Eraut, M. (1995) 'Schon shock: a case for reframing reflection-in action.' *Teachers and Teaching: theory and practice 1*, 1, 9–22.

Erikson, F. (1986) 'Qualitative methods in research on teaching.' In M. Wittrock. *Handbook of Research on Teaching*, 3rd Edition. New York: Macmillan.

Everard, B. and Morris, G. (eds) (1990) *Effective School Management*, 2nd Edition. London: Paul Chapman.

Fielden, J. (1991) 'Resource implications of mergers: are there any economies?' *Higher Education Quarterly 45*, 2, 254–266.

Fieman-Nemser, S. and Floden, R. (1986) 'The cultures of teaching.' In M. Witrock (ed) *Handbook of Research on Teaching*, 3rd Edition. New York: Macmillan.

Finch, J. (1988) 'Ethnography and public policy.' In A. Pollard, J. Purvis and G. Walford (eds) *Education, Training and the New Vocationalism*. Milton Keynes: Open University Press.

Firestone, W. and Corbett, H. (1988) 'Planned organisational change.' In M. Fullan (1991) *The New Meaning of Educational Change*. London: Cassell.

Fisher, K. and Pearson, L. (1995) *Quality Provision in Vocational Education and Training: An Exploratory Study of Tutors' Perspectives*. Research Project Report, School of Education and Health Studies, Bolton Institute of Higher Education.

Fowler, G. (1973) 'Further education.' In R. Bell, G. Fowler and K. Little (eds) *Education in Great Britain and Ireland*. London: Routledge and Kegan Paul.

Frain, J. (1993) *The Changing Culture of a College*. London: Falmer.

Freire, P. (1972) *Pedagogy of the Oppressed*, translated [from the Portuguese] by Myra Bergman Rumos. Harmondsworth: Penguin.

Fryer, B. (1994) 'The core values of adult education.' *Education Today and Tomorrow 46*, 2, 18–19.

Fullan, M. (1990) 'Staff development, innovation, and institutional development.' In B. Joyce (ed) *Changing School Culture Through Staff Development*. Alexandria, Va.: 1990 Yearbook of the Association for Supervision and Curriculum Development.

Fullan, M. (1991) *The New Meaning of Educational Change*. London: Cassell.

Further Education Funding Council (1992) *Funding Learning*. Coventry: FEFC.

Further Education Funding Council (1993a) *Assessing Achievement*, (Circular 93/28). Coventry: FEFC.

Further Education Unit (1991) *Quality Matters: Business and Industry Models and Further Education* London: FEU.

Gadamer, H. (1980) *Truth and Method*, (trans. G. Bardey and J. Cummings). New York: Seabury Press.

Gamble, A. (1988) *The Free Economy and the Strong State: The Politics of Thatcherism*. London: Macmillan.

Garland, P. (1994) 'Using competence-based assessment positively on certificate in education programmes.' *Journal of Further and Higher Education 18*, 2, 16–22.

Getzels, J. and Guba, E. (1957) 'Social behaviour and the administrative process.' *School Review 65*, Winter.

Glaser, B. and Strauss, A. (1965) 'The discovery of substantive theory: a basic strategy underlying qualitative research.' *American Behavioural Scientist 8*, 6, 5–12.

Glaser, B. and Strauss, A. (1966) *Awareness of Dying*. London: Weidenfeld and Nicholson.

Glaser, B. and Strauss, A. (1967) *The Discovery of Grounded Theory*. Chicago: Aldine.

Goodson, I. (1994) 'Studying the teacher's life and work.' *Teaching and Teacher Education 10*, 1, 29–37.

Gore, J. (1993) *The Struggle for Pedagogies*. London: Routledge.

Grace, G. (1993) 'On the study of school leadership: beyond educational management.' *British Journal of Educational Studies 41*, 4, 353–365.

Gray, L. (1992) 'Competition or collaboration – the tensions in colleges of further education.' In T. Simkins, L. Ellison and V. Garrett (eds) *Implementing Educational Reform: The Early Lessons*. Harlow, Essex: Longmans.

Greenfield, T. (1975) 'A theory about organisation: a new perspective and its implications for schools.' In M. Hughes (ed) *Administering Education: International Challenges*. London: Athlone Press of the University of London.

Gretton, I. (1995) 'Taking the lead in leadership.' *Professional Manager 4*, 1, 20–22.

Griffiths, M. (1993) 'Educational change and the self.' *British Journal of Educational Studies 41*, 2, 150–163.

Griffiths, M. and Tann, S. (1991) 'Ripples in the reflection.' In P. Lomax (ed) *Managing Better Schools and Colleges: The Action Research Way*. Clevedon: Multilingual Matters.

Grundy, S. (1989) 'Beyond professionalism.' In W. Carr (ed) *Quality in Teaching: Arguments for a Reflective Profession*. Lewes: The Falmer Press.

Guy, R. (1990) 'Distance education, text and ideology in Papua New Guinea.' *Papua New Guinea Journal of Education 26*, 2, 201–215.

Hall, V. (1987) 'NCVQ and further education.' *Coombe Lodge Report 20*, 5, 285–327.

Hall, V. and Wallace, M. (1993) 'Collaboration as a subversive activity: a professional response to externally imposed competition between schools?' *School Organisation 13*, 2, 101–117.

Hammersley, M. (1993) *Social Research: Philosophy, Politics and Practice*. London: Sage.

Hammersley, M. and Atkinson, M. (1983) *Ethnography: Principles in Practice*. London: Routledge and Kegan Paul.

Hargreaves, A. (1991) 'Contrived collegiality.' In J. Blase (ed) *The Politics of Life in Schools*. London: Sage.

Hargreaves, A. (1993a) 'Individualism and Individuality: reinterpreting the teacher culture.' *International Journal of Educational Research 19*, 2, 227–246.

Hargreaves, A. (1993b) 'Teacher development in the postmodern age: dead certainties, safe simulation and the boundless self.' In P. Gilroy and M. Smith (eds) *International Analyses of Teacher Education, Journal of Education for Teaching, Papers One*. Oxford: Carfax.

Hargreaves, A. (1994) *Changing Teachers, Changing Times: Teachers' Work and Culture in the Postmodern Age*. London: Cassell.

Harvey, L., Burrows, A. and Green, D. (1992) *Criteria of Quality: Summary, Quality in Higher Education Project*. Birmingham: University of Central England.

Hedberg, B., Nystrom, P. and Starbuck, W. (1976) 'Camping on seesaws: prescriptions for a self-designing organisation.' *Administrative Science Quarterly 21*, 1, 41–65.

Hill, G. (ed) (1934) *Boswell's Life of Johnson*, revised edn. L.F. Powell, Entry for 18 April 1775. Oxford: Clarendon Press.

Hodkinson, P. (1992) 'Alternative models of competence in vocational education and training.' *Journal of Further and Higher Education 16*, 2, 30–39.

Hodkinson, P. and Sparkes, A. (1995) 'Markets and vouchers: the inadequacy of individualist policies for vocational education and training in England and Wales.' *Journal of Education Policy 10*, 2, 189–207.

Hopkins, D. (1991) *Self Evaluation and Development Planning as Strategies for School Improvement*. Paper presented to BEMAS 4th Research Conference, Nottingham, April 6–8.

Hoy, W. and Miskel, C. (1989) 'Schools and their external environments.' In R. Glatter (ed) *Educational Institutions and Their Environments: Managing the Boundaries*. Milton Keynes: Open University Press.

Hoyle, E. (1969) *The Role of the Teacher*. London: Routledge and Kegan Paul.

Hoyle, E. (1975) 'Leadership and decision-making in education.' In M. Hughes (ed) *Administering Education: International Challenge*. London: Athlone.

Hoyle, E. (1980) 'Professionalisation and deprofessionalisation in education.' In E. Hoyle and J. Megarry (eds) *The Professional Development of Teachers: World Yearbook of Education*. London: Kogan Page.

Hoyle, E. (1992) *Redefining the Concept of a Profession*. Unpublished Paper given at BEMAS Conference, Bristol.

Huberman, A. (1973) *Understanding Change in Education: An Introduction*. Paris: UNESCO.

Huberman, M. (1990) *The Social Context of Instruction in Schools*. Paper presented to the annual meeting of the American Educational Research Association, Boston, cited in A. Hargreaves (1991) *The Politics of Life in Schools*. London: Sage.

Huberman, M. (1993) *The Lives of Teachers*. London: Cassell.

Hughes, M. (1985) 'Leadership in professionally staffed organisations.' In M. Hughes, P. Ribbins and W. Thomas. *Managing Education: The System and the Institution*. London: Holt, Rinehart and Winston.

Hurst, P. (1987) 'The methodology of qualitative research.' *International Journal of Educational Development 7*, 1, 69–72.

Husen, T. (1974) *The Learning Society*. London: Macmillan.

Hyland, T. (1992a) 'Reconstruction and reform in further education.' *Educational Management and Administration 20*, 2, 106–110.

Hyland, T. (1992b) 'Expertise and competence in further and adult education.' *British Journal of In-Service Education 18*, 1, 23–28.

Hyland, T. (1992c) 'Lecturing: profession or occupation?' *NATFHE Journal, Autumn*, 10–11.

Hyland, T. (1992d) 'The vicissitudes of adult education: competence, epistemology and reflective practice.' *Education Today 42*, 2, 7–12.

Hyland, T. (1993) 'Professional development and competence-based education.' *Educational Studies 19*, 1, 123–132.

Hyland, T. (1994) 'Silk purses and sows ears: NVQs, GNVQs and experiential learning.' *Cambridge Journal of Education 24*, 2, 233–243.

Illich, I. (1973) *Deschooling Society*. Harmondsworth: Penguin.

Johnson, J. (1975) *Doing Field Research*. New York: The Free Press.

Joyce, B. and Showers, B. (1988) *Student Achievement Through Staff Development*. New York: Longman.

Kershaw, N. (1994) 'Unhealthy tendencies.' *Times Educational Supplement* April 15, p.13.

Latcham, J. and Birch, D. (1985) 'Measuring college performance.' *Information Bank Working Paper No 2041*, Coombe Lodge: The Staff College.

Lawn, M. (1989) 'Being caught in schoolwork: the possibilities of research in teachers' work.' In W. Carr (ed) *Quality in Teaching: Arguments for a Reflective Profession*. Lewes: The Falmer Press.

Lawton, D. (1992) *Education and Politics in the 1990s: Conflict or Consensus?* London: Falmer.

Leiberman, A. (ed) (1988) *Building a Professional Culture in Schools.* New York: Teachers College Press.

Leithwood, K. and Jantzi, D. (1990) *Tranformational Leadership: How Principals can Help Reform School Cultures,* Unpublished paper, American Educational Research Association, Boston.

Libby, D. and Hull, R. (1988) 'The LEA, the College and the community.' In B. Kedney and D. Parkes (eds) *Planning the FE Curriculum.* London: Further Education Unit.

Little, J. (1984) 'Seductive images and organisation realities in professional development.' *Teachers' College Record 86,* 1, 84–102, cited in A Hargreaves (1991) *The Politics of Life in Schools.* London: Sage.

Locke, J. ([1690] 1959) *An Essay Concerning Human Understanding,* Two Vols., Edited by A. Fraser. New York: Dover.

Lomas, L. (1993) 'Management competences: the political dimension.' *Journal of Further and Higher Education 17,* 2, 72–76.

McBean, L. (1994) 'Try a little sensitivity.' *The Times Higher,* June 3, page 6.

McCracken, G. (1988) *The Long Interview.* Newbury Park, Ca.: Sage.

McCulloch, M. (1993) 'Democratisation of teacher education: new forms of partnership for school based initial teacher education.' In P. Gilroy and M. Smith. *International Analysis of teacher Education, Journal of Education for Teaching, Papers One.* Oxford: Carfax.

McDonnell, L. and Elmore, R. (1991) 'Getting the job done: alternative policy instruments.' In A. Odden (ed) *Education Policy Implementation.* New York: SUNY Press.

McElwee, G. (1992) 'How useful are performance indicators in the polytechnic sector?' *Educational Management and Administration 20,* 3, 189–192.

McNay, I. and Ozga, J. (1985) *Policy-Making in Education: The Breakdown of Consensus.* Oxford: Pergamon Press.

Macbeth, A., McCreath, D. and Aitchinson, J. (eds) (1995) *Collaborate or Compete? Partnerships in a Market Economy.* London: The Falmer Press.

Maclure, S. (1992, 3rd Edition) *Education Re-formed: A Guide to the Education Reform Act.* London: Hodder and Stoughton.

Malinowski, B. (1922) *Argonauts of the Western Pacific*. London: Routledge and Kegan Paul.

Maslow, A. (1954) *Motivation and Personality*. Harper: New York.

Measor, L. and Woods, P. (1991) 'Breakthroughs and blockages in ethnographic research: contrasting experiences during the Changing Schools project.' In G. Walford (ed) *Doing Educational Research*. London: Routledge.

Merryfield, M. (1993) 'Reflective practice in global education: strategies for teacher educators.' *Theory into Practice 32*, 1, 27–32.

Meyer, J. and Rowan, B. (1988) 'The structure of educational organisations.' In A. Westoby (ed) *Culture and Power in Educational Organisations*. Milton Keynes: Open University Press.

Miles, M. (1987) *Practical Guidelines for School Administrators: How to Get There*, Unpublished paper presented at American Educational Research Association annual meeting, cited in M. Fullan (1991) *The New Meaning of Educational Change*. London: Cassell.

Mill, J. ([1843] 1950) 'A system of logic: ratiocinative and inductive.' Eighth Edition. In E. Nagel (ed) *John Stuart Mill's Philosophy of Scientific Method*. New York: Hafner Press.

Miller, J. and Innis, S. (1990) *Strategic Quality Management: A Working Paper*. Sheffield: Consultants at Work/Training Agency.

Moss, J. (1981) 'Limiting competency based education.' *Studies in Curriculum Research 19*, 1, 14–18.

National Association of Teachers in Further and Higher Education (1994a) 'Sign of the times.' *The Lecturer*, October p.5.

National Council for Vocational Qualifications/Employment Department (1988) *The NVQ Criteria and Related Guidance*. London: NCVQ.

Ozga, J. (1990) 'Policy research and policy theory: a comment on Fitz and Halpin.' *Journal of Education Policy 5*, 4, 359–362.

Ozga, J. (1992) *Teacher Professionalism*, Unpublished paper presented to BEMAS conference, Bristol 1992.

Ozga, J. and Lawn, M. (1981) *Teachers, Professionalism and Class: A Study of Organised Teachers*. London: Falmer.

Ozga, J. and Lawn, M. (1988) 'School work: interpreting the labour process of teaching.' *British Journal of Sociology of Education 9*, 3, 323–336.

Parkes, D. (1991) 'Home thoughts from abroad: diagnosis, prescription and prognosis for British vocational education and training.' *European Journal of Education 26*, 1, 41–53.

Pearsall, M. (1956) 'Participant observation as role and method in behavioral research.' *American Journal of Sociology 65*, 577–584.

Peters, T. (1989) *Thriving on Chaos: Handbook for a Management Revolution*. London: Pan/Macmillan.

Peters, T. and Waterman, R. (1982) *In Search of Excellence: Lessons from America's Best-Run Companies*. New York: Harper and Row.

Pfeffer, J. and Salancik, G. (1978) *The External Control of Organisations: A Resource Dependence Perspective*. New York: Harper Row.

Pietrasik, R. (1987) 'The teachers' action, 1984–1986.' In M. Lawn and G. Grace (eds) *Teachers: The Culture and Politics of Work*. London: The Falmer Press.

Power, S. (1992) 'Researching the impact of education policy: difficulties and discontinuities.' *Journal of Education Policy 7*, 5, 493–500.

Pratley, B. (1980) *Signposts*. London: FEU.

Pring, R. (1976) *Knowledge and Schooling*. London: Open Books.

Pring, R. (1978) 'Teacher as researcher.' In D. Lawton *et al.* (eds) *Theory and Practice of Curriculum Studies*. London: Routledge and Kegan Paul.

Pring, R. (1992) 'Standards and quality in education.' *British Journal of Educational Studies 40*, 1, 4–22.

Raab, C. (1991) *Education Policy and Management: Contemporary Changes in Britain*. Paper presented to International Institute of Administrative Sciences, Copenhagen, July, cited in Ball (1993a) 'Education policy, power relations and teachers' work.' *British Journal of Educational Studies 41*, 2, 106–121.

Ranson, S. (1992) 'Towards the learning society.' *Educational Management and Administration 20*, 2, 68–79.

Ransom, S. (1993) 'Markets or democracy for education.' *British Journal of Educational Studies 41*, 4, 333–352.

Riseborough, G. (1994) 'Teachers' careers and comprehensive school closure: policy and professionalism in practice.' *British Educational Research Journal 20*, 1, 85–104.

Rock, P. (1979) *The Making of Symbolic Interactionism.* London: Macmillan.

Rowan, J. (1981) 'A dialectical paradigm for research.' In P. Reason and J. Rowan (eds) *Human Inquiry.* New York: John Wiley.

Rowan, J. and Reason, P. (1981) 'On making sense.' In P. Reason and J. Rowan (eds) *Human Inquiry.* New York: John Wiley.

Salaman, G. (1979) *Work Organisations: Resistance and Ritual.* London: Longman.

Sallis, E. (1992) 'Total quality management and further education. In T. Simkins, L. Ellison and V. Garrett (eds) *Implementing Educational Reform: The Early Lessons.* Harlow, Essex: Longman.

Satterley, D. (1989 2nd edn) *Assessment in Schools.* Oxford: Basil Blackwell.

Schon, D. (1983) *The Reflective Practitioner: How Professionals Think in Action.* New York: Basic Books.

Schon, D. (1987) *Educating the Reflective Practitioner: Towards a New Design for Teaching and Learning in the Professions.* San Francisco: Jossey-Bass.

Schratz, M. (1993a) 'Researching while teaching: promoting reflective professionality in higher education.' *Educational Action Research 1,* 1, 111–133.

Schratz, M. (1993b) 'Crossing the disciplinary boundaries: professional development through action research in higher education.' *Higher Education Research and Development 12,* 2, 131–142.

Scott, W.R. (1981) *Organisations: Rational, Natural and Open Systems.* Englewood Cliffs, NJ: Prentice Hall.

Selznick, P. (1957) *Leadership in Administration.* New York: Harper Row.

Silver, H. (1990) *Education, Change and the Policy Process.* Lewes, Sussex: Falmer.

Simkins, T., Ellison, L. and Garrett, V. (1992) 'Beyond markets and managerialism: education in a new context.' In T. Simkins, L. Ellison and V. Garrett (eds) *Implementing Educational Reform: The Early Lessons.* Harlow, Essex: Longman.

Singh, B. (1994) 'Human rights, cultural pluralism and education.' *Education Today 44,* 3, 9–15.

Skilbeck, M. (1983) 'Lawrence Stenhouse: research methodology.' *British Educational Research Journal 9*, 1, 11–20.

Smithers, A. (1993) *All Our Futures: Britain's Educational Revolution.* London: Channel 4 Television.

Sockett, H. (1989) 'A moral epistemology of practice.' *Cambridge Journal of Education 19*, 1, 33–39.

Stenhouse, L. (1978) 'Case study and case records: towards a contemporary history of education.' *British Educational Research Journal 4*, 2, 21–39.

Stenhouse, L. (1979a) *Research as a Basis for Teaching.* Inaugural Lecture, Norwich: University of East Anglia.

Stenhouse, L. (1979b) 'Case study in comparative education: particularity and generalisation.' *Comparative Education 15*, 1, 5–11.

Stenhouse, L. (1980) *Curriculum Research and Development in Action.* London: Heinemann.

Stones, E. (1989) 'Pedagogical studies in the theory and practice of education.' *Oxford Review of Education 15*, 1, 3–15.

Theodossin, E. (1982) 'The management of self-interest: phenomenology and staff motivation.' *Coombe Lodge Working Paper IBN 1634.* Bristol: The Further Education Staff College.

Theodossin, E. (1989) *The Responsive College.* Bristol: The Further Education Staff College.

Torrington, D. and Weightman, J. (1989) 'The management of secondary schools.' *Journal of Management Studies 26*, 5.

Training and Development Lead Body (1991) *National Standards for Assessment and Verification of NVQs.* London: TDLB.

Trow, M. (1993) 'The business of learning.' *The Times Higher,* October 8, pages 20–21.

Turner, C. (1990) *Organisational Culture.* Bristol: The Staff College.

Turner, C. (1991) *The Perception of Threat and the Reality of Decline in Organisations.* Bristol: The Staff College.

Twyman, P. (1985) 'Management and leadership in further education.' In M. Hughes, P. Ribbins and H. Thomas. *Managing Education: The System and the Institution.* Eastbourne: Holt, Rinehart and Winston.

Uttley, A. (1994) 'Contracts go unsigned.' *The Times Higher,* April 15 page 3.

Vulliamy, G. and Webb, R. (1992) 'The influence of teacher research: process or product.' *Educational Review 44*, 1, 41–51.

Wagner, J. (1993) 'Educational research as a full participant: challenges and opportunities for generating new knowledge.' *Qualitative Studies in Education 6*, 1, 3–18.

Waitt, I. (ed) (1980) *College Administration*. London: NATFHE.

Wallace, M. (1991) *School Centred Management Training*. London: Paul Chapman.

Walsh, P. (1993) 'Philosophy, education and action research.' *Educational Action Research 1*, 1, 189–191.

Ward, R. (1993) *Consultation on New Contracts for Lecturers and Management Spine Staff Appointed or Promoted after 1 April 1993.* Letter to the Chair of Governors and Principal of each institution preparing for independence, 26 January.

Watts, T. (1993) 'Unbiased?' *Education*, October 8, page 271.

Webb, R. (ed) (1990) *Practitioner Research in the Primary School*. Lewes: Falmer Press.

Weick, K. (1982) 'Administering education in loosely coupled schools.' *Phi Delta Kappan 10*, 673–676.

Weick, K. (1988) 'Educational organisations as loosely coupled systems.' In A. Westoby (ed) *Culture and Power in Educational Organisations*. Milton Keynes: Open University Press.

Weiss, C. (1982) 'Policy research in the context of diffuse decision making.' In D. Kallen *et al.* (eds) *Social Science and Public Policy Making: A Reappraisal*. Windsor: NFER.

West, S. (1996) 'Competition and collaboration in education: marriage not divorce.' In D. Bridges and C. Husbands (eds) *Consorting and Collaborating in the Education Marketplace*. London: The Falmer Press.

West-Burnham, J. (1992) *Managing Quality in Schools*. Harlow: Longmans.

White, C. and Crump, S. (1993) 'Education and the three "P's": policy, politics and practice – a review of the work of S.J. Ball.' *British Journal of Sociology of Education 14*, 4, 415–429.

Whitehead, J. (1989) 'Creating a living educational theory from questions of the kind, "how do I improve my practice?"' *Cambridge Journal of Education 19*, 1, 41–52.

Whyte, W. (1943) *Street Corner Society*. Chicago: University of Chicago Press.

Whyte, W. (1964) 'On street corner society.' In E. Burgess and D. Bogue (eds) *Contributions to Urban Sociology*. Chicago: University of Chicago Press.

Willower, D. (1982) 'School organisations: perspectives in juxtaposition.' *Educational Administration Quarterly 18*, 3.

Subject Index

Names Index